The Crooked Rim

Endorsements

Coach Pam Borton's story of resilience in *The Crooked Rim*, and how it developed through the course of her career and contributed to her success, is a great read and one I promise you will enjoy and take away many practical applications so you can reach your own Final Four.

Sandy Barbour
Vice President for Intercollegiate Athletics
Penn State University

I highly recommend *The Crooked Rim*. As a corporate leader and now in the NFL, my experience highlights the one common denominator in every great leader: resilience. This book is a powerful resource to help build the much-needed muscle of resilience for any corporate athlete who wants to get to the next level.

Karin Nelsen
Executive Vice President & Chief Legal Officer
Minnesota Vikings Football, LLC

Resilience and mental toughness go hand in hand with great leadership. *The Crooked Rim* explores the development of these skills and celebrates the value they will add to the skill portfolio of any leader. For those looking to enhance their leadership mindset, *The Crooked Rim* should be required reading.

Lisa Brummel
Co-Owner, Seattle Storm (WNBA)
Former Executive and Chief People Officer, Microsoft

Pam Borton's wisdom and advice in *The Crooked Rim* is as enduring as a handmade coat passed down through a family. It's practical, of high quality and, most importantly, comes from a place of love—for life, its challenges, and all the opportunities it offers."

Chief Todd Axtell
Chief of Police
St. Paul (Minnesota) Police Department

The Crooked Rim reminds us that mastering our mindset and building mental toughness are important skills for all leaders. My work with Pam Borton helped rebuild my confidence and taught me to use intentional scorekeeping and self-coaching strategies to bolster my resilience. I continue this practice every day! I make mistakes, but mental toughness keeps me focused to improve my "free throw" on my own crooked rim. This is a must-read for all leaders!

Lin Hillis
Associate Vice President—Talent, Leadership & Diversity
The Ohio State University

Pam Borton has every quality a great coach must possess, and she shares her journey of resilience and practical tools for success in *The Crooked Rim*. Coaching elite athletes, NCAA teams and staffs, and CEOs and executive teams, she knows what it takes to build resilience and mental toughness to lift high performers to the next level. Successful leaders must become coaches themselves, focusing beyond today's game and leading the way through life-long learning, growth, and development. The best athletes—sports and corporate—have the best coaches around them and Pam is the indispensable coach we all need in our huddles.

Gene DeFilippo
Senior Managing Director, Turnkey Sports
Former Director of Athletics, Villanova University
and Boston College

I highly recommend both of Pam Borton's books—*ON POINT and The Crooked Rim*—to anyone who faces adversity in the workplace or in life. Pam's guidance as my coach enabled me to remain resilient through a difficult situation and to strengthen my emotional intelligence, ultimately transforming me into a better leader.

Michelle Orner
SC Quality Control Manager
PepsiCo

Pam Borton leverages her keen perspective and experience in *The Crooked Rim* to help lift others to heights that they did not think possible. Having benefited from her coaching personally, I was able to navigate through a career transformation which required resilience to accomplish my goals.

Bryan Laskin, DDS
Chief Executive Officer
OperaDDS

Coach Pam Borton's *The Crooked Rim* lays the foundation of 'must do's' for anyone leading and building teams in today's tumultuous arena. Taking us along on her own journey, both professional and personal, she lights the path for the realization of one's own limitless life. Whatever your Final Four looks like, know it requires strengthening you and your team's resiliency, laid out expertly in her step-by-step building blocks for the journey, helping all of us to achieve our greatest heights.

Jennifer L. Kraschnewski, MD, MPH
Vice Chair of Clinical Research, Department of Medicine
Penn State College of Medicine

Pam Borton is THE expert on mental toughness. As humans, we naturally encounter significant stress in our lives—and sometimes it seems life continues to pile challenges on us all at once. Pam's coaching strategies using the resilience tools in *The Crooked Rim* help to overcome the punches that life brings us all. Pam has helped me navigate rough seas by strengthening my relationships and mindfulness to become an influential leader who not only exceeds expectations, but also calms the rough waters with grace.

Tana McDermott
Vice President, Revenue Operations
Workiva, Inc.

In a business world focused on using industrial logic to persevere over adversity, resilience is the light. If there was ever a time to get mentally tough, this is it! *The Crooked Rim* is a perfect weapon to combat the adversity in today's world. Pam Borton gives you the keys to success in a guide that doesn't sugar coat the mental toughness required to reach your goals. To today's leaders and our next generation, please take this playbook and run. This book will guide you to be mentally strong and give you the tools to lead others through adversity.

Bob Erdle
Chief Revenue Officer
Four Winds Interactive

The Crooked Rim is an indispensable resource! When my husband was severely injured in an accident that suddenly changed our lives, I had to dig deep and master keeping a positive mindset. Staying strong for my family and continuing to meet the demands of my role as a CFO took daily effort and focus. Pam Borton helped me develop a positive mindset and build my resilience so I can continue to be successful.

Chris Norring
Chief Financial Officer
FORCE America, Inc.

I have read so much on the topic of leadership, but my work with Pam Borton eclipses every other source I have consumed. Pam understands the nuanced necessities leadership requires, and she helps eliminate distractions that divert you from investing in the strategies and tactics to continuously improve your ability to lead with purpose and to ignite positive action. Read *The Crooked Rim*—you'll transform your life.

Joel Capperella
Vice President, Product Marketing
Workiva, Inc.

Finding your way to define and to build resilience is a path not many of us travel. We have dreams and goals, and our guts tell us there is a path of success. Coach Pam Borton knows how to guide us to understand our own mindsets, learn life lessons, and to let go of what holds us back. *The Crooked Rim* will help you stay true to your path regardless of the obstacles.

Shauna Bryngelson, CPDM
Principal—Life, Absence and Disability
Mercer, Inc.

Pam Borton's experience and expertise put her in the ranks of some of the most influential coaches of athletes and corporate leaders. She presses her clients and teams to get comfortable being uncomfortable: embracing and learning from failure and changing their mindsets. In *The Crooked Rim*, Pam provides practical strategies for mastering our mindset, building inner strength and resilience, and developing the mental toughness we all need to accomplish big things. This book will energize you . . . get ready to be inspired!

Hillary Eckert
Vice President, Integrated Risk
Workiva, Inc.

Without a doubt, *The Crooked Rim* is a powerful and awe-inspiring guide that will benefit every leader and the teams and communities they serve. The insights, strategies, and approaches offered will help you activate and enhance necessary and vital leadership competencies. Next-level leaders will find *The Crooked Rim* a must-read (and a must re-read!).

Katrice A. Albert, PhD
Founder & Managing Member
Third Eye Consulting Group, LLC

Mastering my mindset and strengthening my resilience has allowed me to flourish. Pam Borton is a resilient, perceptive, and gifted leadership coach who helped me navigate adversity, setbacks, and obstacles. This book provides the tools and strategies Pam has shared with me first-hand. Let it serve as your guide to gain confidence to form a clear path for your own success and to accomplish your dreams.

Michelle Amato
Vice President of Sales, Global Financial Services
Workiva, Inc.

THE
CROOKED
RIM

Master Your Mindset to Strengthen
Your Resilience for Limitless Personal
and Professional Excellence

PAM BORTON

NEW YORK

LONDON • NASHVILLE • MELBOURNE • VANCOUVER

THE CROOKED RIM

Master Your Mindset to Strengthen Your Resilience for Limitless Personal and Professional Excellence

Published in New York, New York, by Morgan James Publishing. Morgan James is a trademark of Morgan James, LLC. www.MorganJamesPublishing.com

Ordering Information:
Quantity sales. Special discounts are available on quantity purchases by corporations, associations, and others. For details, contact the publisher at the address above. Orders by U.S. trade bookstores and wholesalers. Please contact Morgan James Publishing Tel: (800) 800-8000; Fax: (800) 800-8001.

Proudly distributed by Ingram Publisher Services.

Morgan James BOGO™

A **FREE** ebook edition is available for you or a friend with the purchase of this print book.

CLEARLY SIGN YOUR NAME ABOVE

Instructions to claim your free ebook edition:
1. Visit MorganJamesBOGO.com
2. Sign your name CLEARLY in the space above
3. Complete the form and submit a photo of this entire page
4. You or your friend can download the ebook to your preferred device

ISBN 9781631956010 paperback
ISBN 9781631956034 ebook
ISBN 9781631956027 hardcover
Library of Congress Control Number:
2021940012

Cover and Interior Design by:
Chris Treccani
www.3dogcreative.net

Morgan James PUBLISHING **Builds** *with...* **Habitat for Humanity** Peninsula and Greater Williamsburg

Morgan James is a proud partner of Habitat for Humanity Peninsula and Greater Williamsburg. Partners in building since 2006.

Get involved today! Visit MorganJamesPublishing.com/giving-back

IN MEMORY OF MY YOUNGER SISTER, LISA
*"For love is eternal, and those we love shall
be with us throughout all eternity."*

AND TO MY PARENTS, RUTH ANN AND LARRY
*For my wonderful upbringing on the farm,
for instilling my values, and for their unconditional love*

TABLE OF CONTENTS

FOREWORD

The road to a resilient life is bumpy with many twists and turns. Around every corner the proverbial "punch in the nose" waits to lay you out flat. And "crooked rims" conspire to keep your best shots from putting you on the scoreboard at work, at home, and in the community.

A life of leadership and purpose is a full-contact sport and resilience is one of the critical tools that you need to nurture and to carry with you to lead the most successful, meaningful, and enjoyable life possible. Resilience, at its core, is about belief in oneself and about a belief in contributing to something larger than you. In *The Crooked Rim*, leader and Coach Pam Borton shares a career's worth of winning leadership experience, advice, and strategies to nurture and to grow your capacity for resilience, to address the adversity that life will inevitably throw your way.

We all have some level of capacity to pick ourselves up when we are down—to get back in the game after a setback—and Coach Borton's real-life experience, expertise, and strategies show us that each of us can grow a resilient response capacity and be better prepared for that next twist, turn, punch, and crooked rim. Fortunately, resilience can be learned, developed, and cultivated over time.

As we navigate a world beset by a public health crisis, social injustice, economic inequity, and social media influence threatening to compromise our values on almost every meaningful subject, our ability to have a clear purpose, steadfast resolve, and an uncommon resilience is critical not only for professional success, but for personal fulfillment and joy. I am convinced that a positive attitude, an abundance of gratitude, and a growth mindset are critical to acquire the sense of mastery and confidence that contribute immensely to resilience.

Sports presents an ideal platform to examine resilience because of its balance of the physical, mental, and emotional. Every day, the scoreboard, the opponent, or the mere thought of the next competitive encounter test those of us who work in and compete in sports. We succeed and fail multiple times a day—every day, every week, every month, every year. These tussles with adversity help us to develop and to sharpen our resilience continually. It is not about avoiding adversity; it is about developing the skills to accept the positive gifts adversity is meant to offer us, to resist the temptation to dwell on the detrimental elements, and to keep moving forward, made better by every challenging situation.

Enjoy this compelling journey with Coach Borton. She has lived every minute of it, from the farm and crooked rim, to the NCAA Final Four, to a successful entrepreneurial and executive coaching career. Her story of resilience, and how it developed through the course of her career and contributed to her success, is a great read and one I promise you will enjoy and take away many practical applications so you can reach your own Final Four.

Sandy Barbour
Vice President for Intercollegiate Athletics
Penn State University
"The Unrelenting" Most Influential and Most Outstanding Women in Sports, *Sports Illustrated*
2017 Athletic Director of the Year, Under Armour
Top 25 Most Powerful People in College Sports, *Forbes*
100 Most Influential Women in Business,
San Francisco Business Times

INTRODUCTION

From the Barn to the
Boardroom . . . and Beyond

*"So often in life things that you regard as an impediment
turn out to be great, good fortune."*
–Ruth Bader Ginsburg–

I begin this book with an open and honest confession: writing
is not easy for me and writing a book is downright daunting. I share this with you to help you understand the powerful
force that compels me to write about resilience and mental toughness. These topics are compelling enough, important enough, and
widespread enough for me to put pen to paper for a second time,
following up on my first book, *On Point*. Ironically, writing about
resilience demanded me to demonstrate my own resilience.

Think of *The Crooked Rim* as both a time warp and a time
capsule. It is a time warp for me, because "resilience" was not a

part of our collective vocabulary when I was a child taking shot after shot, day after day at the crooked basketball rim nailed to our family farm's old barn. And it is a time capsule, because whether you read this book during the global pandemic, in the aftermath of a polarizing presidential election, and rising social injustice or reflect back a decade (or more) later, you will understand that not only did these issues spread like the virus, but so did the concepts of resilience and mental toughness.

To write about these critical skills, I needed to create an optimal environment to strengthen my own resilience and mental toughness—namely to eliminate distractions and sharpen my focus. I spent four weeks nestled in the Sierra Nevada mountains writing 10 to 12 hours a day, savoring a private and productive writing retreat. Each day I was inspired by beautiful views of Lake Tahoe and Diamond Peak, the local ski hill in Incline Village, Nevada. I became part of this fabulous community and was a frequent patron at the local coffee shop, *Drink Coffee Do Stuff* . . . which quickly became my daily mantra. They had the best vibe, with café music and delicious harvest muffins as a treat and motivation for writing each day. I called the people at ACE Hardware by name and relished daily yoga and my morning runs on the famous lakeshore boulevard.

Knowing that running outdoors provided fuel for my productivity and creative mindset, I started each day with a five-mile run on the flattest running trail I could find in the aptly named Incline Village at 6,350 feet above sea level. I learned quickly that the five-mile stretch along Lakeshore Boulevard is a playground for the mega-wealthy, with an abundance of multi-million-dollar mansions that overlook Lake Tahoe. Even the dogs, sporting bling-bling collars, looked well-to-do. After a long day of writing, I left the ski chalet and drove down the mountain to the Tahoe east shore trailhead to end my day and to clear my mind with a peaceful walk.

There were many disturbing events that happened throughout 2020, but the Presidential Election dominated the nation's consciousness and the daily round-the-clock news cycle. There was no escape. We all were deeply affected by all these events; however, the election drama broke the camel's back. With seven inches of snow falling outside, I will admit that I was having a visceral experience alone at the ski chalet. I felt mentally and emotionally tested—a return to the anxiety and stress I felt during some of the biggest collegiate basketball games I coached. My mindset, resilience, and mental toughness were highjacked and I was spiraling out of control. Alone and isolated, the divisiveness and the magnitude of hate that poured out in our great country took a toll and challenged my health, vitality, and core values.

I struggled and hit rock bottom emotionally. I broke down high up in the Sierra mountains, 2,200 miles from home. I watched in disbelief, and with anger, those we call our "leaders"; the deep hate and divisiveness in our country also created many challenges within my own family. I was struggling and in disbelief, losing my grip and questioning my white-picket fence upbringing. I was raised believing in reality, love, faith, kindness, and respect as my values, and all I could see and hear were the opposite. During times of crisis, our true colors either shine like a beacon of light or darken the light in others. I felt overwhelmed and knew I needed to change my mindset and to put my own strategies into play immediately.

One of the greatest benefits of resilience and mental toughness integrating into our collective vocabulary, is that is gives us a common language and foundation on which to build. There is a common saying: If you can name it, you can claim it." That is exactly what I did. Not only could I recognize the feelings I was experiencing, but I could implement effective strategies to get myself unstuck and to move forward.

Our mind represents our most powerful tool and, just like how yoga and running strengthen the body, we must train it every day. That way, when challenges, difficulties, and setbacks show up in life, adversity motivates and fuels you, like it does for me. We have a choice: crawl up in a fetal position and wait for the storm to pass or dig deep into our internal toolkit filled with resilience and mental toughness and pass through the storm to the other side. Instead of waiting or relying on someone else to toss you a life preserver if you are drowning, know that you always have the ability, the strength, and the know-how to save yourself . . . that is grit, that is resilience, and that is mental toughness. Whether we win or lose in a traditional sense, we strive to fail with grace or to prevail with humility. Either way, we are victorious, and either way, we know we will be ok.

For the elite players and now corporate athletes I coach, the training process never ends. There is always room for improvement and opportunities to grow, especially when it comes to resilience, well-being, and mental health. Life will always present adversities, hard times, hardships, disappointments, and curveballs we need to navigate. For many reasons, mental health issues have become one of the greatest challenges impacting people of all ages and all walks of life. For decades and generations, mental health has been a crisis and only now are we beginning not only to talk about it, but to understand and to employ coaching strategies and mechanisms to deal with it.

We do not lack the courage, just the knowledge of how to train and to master our mindset to navigate the modern world and all its complexities. We need an updated "how-to" manual and roadmap with better strategies and approaches to deal with uncertainty and to face the unknown. *The Crooked Rim* shares stories starting with the crooked basketball rim nailed to my family's Ohio barn, through my journey coaching collegiate sports, and into the boardroom.

We all face "crooked rims" throughout our personal and professional lives when things are extra hard and there are extra bumps in the road . . . some of us with greater frequency or magnitude than others. No matter what your crooked rim looks like, you must take ownership and responsibility for your own learning, development, and decisions. In the end, no one will do it for you. Step up and break through your limits. Turn *your* crooked rim into your greatest success story.

People reach out to me daily, believing their C-suite titles, multiple degrees, credentials, and positions of wealth should guarantee them everlasting fulfillment. Yet, these same individuals face tremendous stress, anxiety, burnout, depression, and uncertainty in their lives just like everyone else. There is no "get out of jail free" card. These stories and their responses are all too common. We read the research and statistics, and observe the breakdown in our conventional beliefs, as we struggle to address the complexities of life and to define what success means to each of us. While the work to gain clarity is difficult, the dual victory of self-awareness and self-efficacy is worth the fight.

I am honored that people open up to me—whether by virtue of "knowing" me from my book ON POINT or recognizing my coaching background—yet so many of us never share our fears and anxieties with anyone in our lives. We tend to endure the battle alone and try to keep a stiff upper lip in public. While we perceive tremendous pressure for perfection and to present a flawless façade, in reality there are cracks in every foundation and everyone just tries their best to keep the dam from breaking. Stagnation in life or at work, and finding ourselves lost on the journey, create enormous shame because we operate with broken assumptions. Some of us "earn it" by just grinding it out, but others find themselves in impossible situations with an expectation to get out of the rut alone and without help or direction. Life is not meant to be a solo sport, but a team sport.

Our history overflows with stories demonstrating how individuals, teams, organizations, and institutions rise to the challenge. We also have experienced personal loss and watched others crumble. A crisis separates good leaders from the rest, stretching and putting true resilience and mental toughness to the test. Leaders who model a mindset of resilience make the difference in a crisis—and every day, no matter the situation.

It is survival of the fittest and resilient leaders will rise to the top during a crisis. People crave vulnerable, calm, inspirational, relatable, and thoughtful leaders. Rapidly evolving and unpredictable conditions present an opportunity to develop and to practice empathy, adaptability, self-awareness, and strategic thinking. We must have the capability to think strategically into the future, to develop self-awareness, and to lead with empathy. We must be able to connect with and understand our own purpose, the purpose of the company, and what elements deliver value to all stakeholders in the future. Many new leaders have said the pandemic has been their "baptism by fire".

In addition to operational action, many leaders have leveraged the health and business crisis as an opportunity to strengthen the belief in what is possible, for themselves and others. In five years, leaders will roll up their sleeves, show the "scars" from the crisis, and tell others: You wish you would have been there. Leaders who embraced the challenges are better prepared to create new and powerful opportunities. Today's scars are tomorrow's stripes. This is a great time to lead. Others have missed the speeding train and remain stuck at the station.

Life expects a lot from us. Being physically fit allows us to live; being mentally fit allows us to thrive. To perform at high levels over the long haul, we must develop healthy habits and practice resilience-boosting skills every day. The more we train and practice them, the better we become at dealing with stress, burnout, and fatigue, and which enables us to eliminate many derailers in our lives. *The Crooked Rim* offers a comprehensive, yet simple, approach and proven techniques for those who face unprecedented obstacles and daily demands, personally and professionally.

I have learned not only how to differentiate those who grow after failure from those who will burnout or collapse, but also how to empower the people who have collapsed (or will) with the skills they need to thrive. I have worked with colleagues from around the world to develop skills and competencies for resilience and mental toughness. Some of these individuals have struggled with serious mental wellness issues such as depression and post-traumatic stress disorder (PTSD); yet, many of them have experienced post-traumatic growth and opportunity. My goal is to instill a resilient mindset in individuals through training—instead of through struggling—and to increase the number of those who grow and reach the next level. We have the ability to create an army who can turn their most difficult moments and experiences into catalysts for growth and improved performance.

The ability to bounce back from stress and adversity is important throughout life, especially as we mature and face many transitions, such as health problems, job loss, financial stress, home-life changes, loss of loved ones, and isolation or separation from our children and family. How we adjust to these changes helps determine what we can achieve in life moving forward and how we can increase our own fulfillment, happiness, and well-being.

Resilience and mental toughness relate directly. The outcome is subtly different but significant in a world where everyone experiences change, challenge, and setbacks more frequently and more quickly than ever before. When we are resilient, we bounce back (some quicker than others) from adversity and failure. When we adopt a mentally tough, positive mindset, we are "comfortable in our own skin" and accept life's ups and downs as part of the journey, rolling with the punches and carrying on steadfastly. Both capabilities—the recovery of resilience and the mindset of mental toughness—are critical to success.

We all have "crooked rims" in our lives. For high performers, too often, these challenges hinder our ability to "sink the game-winning shot". But it does not have to be that way; it is tragic if the crooked rim becomes the singular obstacle that keeps us from sinking the shot. Instead, think of the crooked rim as a gift—an opportunity to release us from what holds us back and it makes us tougher. Without the crooked rim, we may never break through and break out. Without the crooked rim, we may never know what we are really made of and how strong we really are. We cannot control the challenges that crooked rims may pose, but we can choose how we respond mentally and emotionally.

This book represents my desire to inspire hope, to build confidence, and to spread my powerful belief that resilience and mental toughness are attainable for anyone. It is right there within your grasp . . . just reach for it. For more than 30 years, I have coached these principles and taken elite players and now corporate athletes to their own Final Fours. You can do it, too.

Consider *The Crooked Rim* your personal playbook to master your mindset for success! It is filled with real-life experiences, positive psychology and well-being exercises, emotional intelligence insights, best practices, and successes and failures—everything you need to build greater resilience. You will learn practical tools and strategies to master a tougher mindset, strengthen personal resilience, develop resilient teams, and perform like an elite corporate athlete to manage elevated expectations and insurmountable stress. Now more than ever, these are the most critical skills needed at home and at work. These strategies have populated my personal playbook over the course of my life, and I have shared them with my players, my high-performing clients, audiences, and now with you. I hope they will make a difference and a positive impact in your life—and in the lives of those around you.

Remember, your mind is the most powerful muscle in the body, and it can either propel you to new heights or prevent you from fulfilling your dreams. The language you use, stories you tell yourself and others, and your beliefs pave the road to success—or to struggle. Your core beliefs guide every aspect of your life, positively and negatively. Fortunately, you have control over your own mind. Mastering my mindset has been a powerful source of strength in my own growth and development, and it is my sincere wish that it will do the same for you.

The Crooked Rim will inspire and motivate you and help you realize you are worth the hard work. As famed Green Bay Packer coach Vince Lombardi said, "The price of success is hard work, dedication to the job at hand, and the determination that whether we win or lose, we have applied the best of ourselves to the task at hand."

I am honored that you have welcomed me as your coach on this journey and I am excited to help you, your team, and your organization get to the next level and experience your own Final Four. LET'S GO!

PART 1

THE JOURNEY

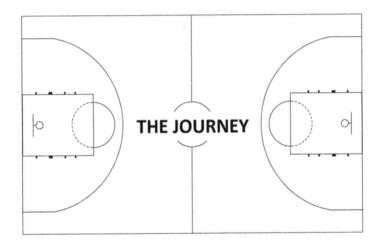

1

The Crooked Rim

"I've never tried to block out memories of the past, even though some are painful. I don't understand people who hide from their past. Everything you live through helps to make you the person you are now."
–SOPHIA LOREN–

I closed my eyes and I was standing on the free throw line, focusing on a rusted, crooked rim. Like traveling in a time machine, I was transported immediately from the University of Minnesota arena (familiarly known as The Barn) back to the Ohio farm where I grew up. The buzz of the crowd in The Barn receded and my mind settled into comforting thoughts of my early childhood, where my experiences and family values created the emotional and mental framework for resilience that continues with me today.

Frame of Mind

Our farm raised pigs and cattle, cultivated corn and wheat, and had one of the biggest gardens you could ever imagine. My Mom truly had a magical "green thumb", or at least she thought she did. We always had fresh vegetables, sweet corn, strawberries, rhubarb, and an array of the most colorful flowers that popped up annually in the garden. My favorite was fresh rhubarb, especially when my mom made rhubarb custard pie. Growing up, our daily food supply was farm to table just like today's best restaurants.

We were not well off financially, but we always had enough to get by. We had everything we needed to accomplish anything we set our minds to achieve. Mom made some of our clothes on her sewing machine or she would find a lovely shirt or dress at a garage sale. When we grew out of our clothes, we would pass them down so all four girls could wear these glorious gems. We shared tight quarters in a mobile home, and my sisters were my roommates until I was 11 years old. The four of us bunked together in a single room with one closet, two beds, and a small bathroom we shared with our mom and dad. It was neither ideal nor idyllic, but it was a very loving home.

I would not trade my upbringing for anything; it defined me and embedded my values. As a result of the limitations and challenges I faced as a child, I learned the importance of developing limitless resilience, strengthening it continuously, and applying it throughout my life. Quitting was never an option on the farm. The expectation that later became my mantra was "just find a way." From sunrise to sunset, my life on the farm instilled an indefatigable work ethic and a goal- and success-oriented mindset that created my foundation for success—no matter the circumstances.

As I stood in "The Barn" at Williams Arena with my eyes closed on the free throw line, my mind could clearly see the crooked rim nailed to the side of our own red barn on our family's Ohio farm. The rusted rim was made of lighter steel which made it bend easily. My dad had taken a piece of plywood, painted it to match the fire engine red barn, and nailed it to the side of the barn as the backboard. The rim never had a net and it did not meet the regulation height of 10 feet. The "court" was a crabgrass surface with dirt, small stones, and a few potholes.

The hog pen lay on the other side of the red barn. On a hot, windy day, the odor of hundreds of hogs created a nauseating stench that would take your breath away. I could feel the rubber basketball in my hands as I spun it. I automatically calculated the adjustment on my shot, bent my knees slightly, and drew in my breath with hope. I took a shot and it clanged off the back of the crooked rim, dropping off to the side. I mumbled a foul word at the missed shot and I quickly glanced over my shoulder at the open kitchen window as the curtain danced with the evening breeze. I felt relieved my mom did not hear me as I bounced forward to retrieve the ball. The ball hopped over some sticks as it picked up speed before stopping in small pothole.

I loved to shoot and that crooked rim served as a friend . . . and a nemesis. Getting the ball through that rim was a battle I embraced every day. I had to adjust and adapt my focus, aim, and strategy on every shot. Shooting at a crooked rim was always challenging, deciding where to stand, calculating how to aim, and assessing the backboard and where the ball might fit through the widest part of the rim. Most days, you could find me trying to beat the crooked rim late into the dark of the night, with a single farm spotlight providing the only light.

Most of us do not grow up with gold-standard gear or state-of-the-art equipment. My used basketball was bright orange, a rubber outdoor Rawlings ball. My mother found the ball at a flea market in Indiana and it always had a slow leak. The uneven basketball court never guaranteed a true bounce as I tried to dribble on the grass, stones, and potholes. It was a perfect training ground for adaptability and resilience—and for life.

I picked up the ball and, without hesitating, banked a short jumper that thudded off the wooden backboard. My shot was on point as it dropped through the crooked rim. *Take that you crooked rim . . . you did not beat me this time!* I dribbled to the faded grass that marked the free-throw line as daylight turned to dusk. The old farm spotlight clicked on; that meant supper was almost ready. I could still squeeze in a few more shots before I devoured the meal and dove into my mom's freshly baked sugar cookies for dessert.

I started counting down . . . 6 . . . 5 . . . 4 . . . 3 . . . 2 . . . and I took the last shot in the game. I fired a turn-around jumper at the crooked rim and imagined the crowd going crazy. As the ball dropped through, the announcer shouted, *Borton beats the buzzer . . . !* The crooked rim did not win tonight and I pumped my fist and ran to the house. As I washed my hands before supper, I could still imagine the celebration in the locker room after the game. I ran to the table and ate quickly so I could go back outside.

My favorite time to work on my craft was at night under the farm spotlight. The old light was attached to a tall pole that lit up the crooked rim. The spotlight resembled a lighthouse beacon, bathing the area in white light while everything else remained pitch black. On this court, I learned to accept things the way they are and not to get frustrated, but to embrace unpredictable and imperfect conditions as challenges and motivators. This mindset and outlook that began as a daily battle with a crooked rim became a driving force for how I am wired and who I am today.

My Dad knew all along that he was teaching me to be more resilient and to be tougher. He tried to bend the rim back into a more cylinder-like shape, but the pounding only made the rim worse. In that frustrating moment, I realized that our "rims" will never be perfect and that our "shots" do not always turn out the way we imagine. We will face adversity disguised as disappointments, setbacks, losses, speed bumps, and curve balls. As a child, I always disagreed with Dad that shooting at a crooked rim would somehow sharpen my game—but it did more than that. The crooked rim was my opportunity, daily training camp, and teacher of one of my most power life lessons: the critical importance of resilience and the effort required to build it. For that, I say, *Thank you, crooked rim (and Dad!).*

> **We will face adversity disguised as disappointments, losses, setbacks, speed bumps, and curve balls. To compete in life, we must strengthen our resilience daily.**

I felt a nudge at my elbow and was jolted back to reality by one of my team managers who said, *Hey Coach, here is the game plan.* It was loud and raucous at The Barn in Williams Arena. The Stanford Cardinal women's basketball team was in town for a big nonconference match-up. This was a true test and a golden opportunity to beat a high-ranked opponent. Like many coaches, the comfort of a rolled-up game plan, program, or towel provided a "security blanket" as I paced up and down the sideline during the game.

My legs felt like they were cemented to the floor and the butterflies in my stomach felt as big as bats. The pep band was playing, the fans were on their feet, and the colors of the Minnesota

Golden Gophers and Stanford Cardinal were bright. My emotions were as intense as the smell of popcorn, colorful sights of the teams, and rising excitement of the fans. I smiled as I cleared the flashback of the crooked rim . . . I was fired up and ready to go.

The Big Ten officials came over to shake my hand as I mumbled under my breath to wake up. Everyone was watching every move I made on the sideline. I smiled and gave high-fives to the players heading off the floor after their warm-up. I turned and looked at the digital scoreboard suspended over center court; the clock was ticking down with just under a minute before the pre-game buzzer sounded. My heart and adrenaline were pumping, experiencing the rush that all players and coaches feel at game time.

I realize now that I had been preparing for big moments—Final Four moments—my entire life. And I know that my experiences and mental toughness have built the resilience necessary to perform under pressure and to embrace challenging situations. Not everyone will coach a Final Four game, but everyone will face stressful moments. Today, in addition to the typical struggles that show up in our personal and professional lives, a global pandemic has hit like an endless tsunami overwhelming us with one crisis after another—physical ailments, emotional turmoil, financial instability, social restrictions, and political upheaval.

Whether you are dealing with daily drama or a deadly virus, resilience and mental toughness are the tools you need to not only survive but to thrive during difficult times. They are the tools you must have in your toolbox before you need to use them; you should implement daily strategies to build and to strengthen your resilience so it stands ready when you need it. Think of it like the bench player who trains for hours every day to improve their ball-handling skills, their endurance, and their free throws so when the coach tells them to take the winning shot, they are confident and ready to win.

Strengthening resilience and developing mental toughness do not happen overnight; they develop through proven coaching strategies, an ongoing commitment to personal growth and development, and an unwavering belief that you can do it. My rusty, crooked rim was not just a metaphor for developing a happy, productive outlook on life. The countless hours I spent honing my shot and sharpening my skills under less-than-ideal conditions galvanized the belief I have in myself.

In truth, my story is not unique. Everyone has a story and a crooked rim of their own—an opportunity to flex that muscle and become bigger, faster, and stronger. My clients learn and practice the skills to improve, and so can you.

Caroline's Crooked Rim

Caroline was a high performer at a global technology company. In fact, she was the top sales leader every year by twice as much as the runner-up. Caroline also was the only female sales representative in the company. As her coach, I quickly realized that she had been shooting at a crooked rim for several years. The only female in the sales department, Caroline was paid a lower base salary than her male counterparts, while sales dashboards validated that her peers were delivering half the results. She travelled three weeks out of the month, mentored several sales reps across the organization, exceeded goals and expectations in every way, and learned how to elevate her confidence and to use her voice. She consistently went above and beyond in every way.

Caroline swam competitively in college and she brought the same drive to her career. In addition to setting new sales records year after year, she aspired to have a seat at the executive table, demonstrating unwavering confidence, advocating for herself and others, and learning how to coach her own team effectively. She faced a crooked rim daily as others held her down instead of lifting her up. She was excluded from meetings, did not get invited to after-work happy hours with the guys, and co-workers mocked her success. She was at the top of the leader board every quarter—yet there were no promotions in the near future. Her goals and dreams were bigger and she knew want she wanted. She faced difficult shots on a crooked rim every day with no clear career path, broken promises, pay inequity, and limited resources.

Caroline shot at her crooked rim for several years without giving up and without giving in. I recognized the same passion, drive, ambition, and desire to be the best that I saw in myself. She was resilient and a winner with a proven track record and a laser-focus on joining the C-suite one day. We discussed the obstacles, potholes, and brick walls that were trying to derail and to discourage her from achieving her goals. Together, we explored the qualities Caroline would need to make her dreams come true. The qualities did not include more cold-calling or a better closing ratio to improve sales; they included persistence, patience, impulse control, grit, belief, and confidence to improve her resilience and mental toughness. Her crooked rim continues to surface, and it looks different at every turn and at every level, even as she succeeds in breaking through the barriers.

While adversity did not cease to exist in her life and work, Caroline continues a daily practice to strengthen her resilience and to develop a more consistent mindset, confidence, and courage. Metaphorically, the crooked rim can appear in a variety of shapes, sizes, situations, and circumstances. I was reminded of this again with my client, Cole.

Cole's Crisis of Confidence

Cole dedicated 22 years to serving our country in the military and was deployed four times to Iraq and Afghanistan following 9-11. He retired after a decorated career and was climbing the ladder in his second career, as a senior level leader for one of the largest organizations on the East Coast. In his role, he led project teams implementing updated technology for an old and outdated system.

Cole was thriving and his performance was firing on all cylinders. He was respected, had strong relationships across the organization, and had great reviews from peers. Then his long-time supervisor retired, the CEO was let go, and the organization went through two interim CEOs over an 18-month period. You can imagine what happened from there. With unstable leadership from the top over a long period of time, the culture descended into chaos. The organization was broken and Cole got caught in the middle, reporting to four different supervisors in 18 months. He lost his confidence, his team, his true north, and his hope.

Cole needed to rediscover himself. It was critical to help Cole regain his confidence, redefine his role, and identify his purpose and the value he brought to his team. We spent time recalling and revisiting past successes, reconfirming his natural skills and strengths, and rebuilding his sense of self-worth. He told me about a time when he was deployed in Afghanistan, when he was performing at his peak. He described the event in detail, who was with him, the circumstances, and the outcome that resulted from performing at an optimal level. After an hour, he was beaming and sitting straight up in his chair. I asked what he could take from that experience and how he could apply it to the chaos and doubt he had as a leader in this organization. He identified several action steps and strategies he could implement immediately.

I was inspired by Cole's story. I leaned in and said, *Cole, you should feel so confident and fulfilled in what you have already accomplished in your life. You have nothing more to prove to anyone. Look what you have done throughout your life. Hold your head up high— you have done so much for this organization and for your country. You have led troops in foxholes, you have carried your teammates off the field, you have saved lives and led teams from diverse backgrounds. You have accomplished more than most people could ever dream. What you are experiencing now is not your fault. Remember who you are and what you have accomplished. Be proud and get back in the game and play at your highest level.* Cole was silent, then he smiled as a tear rolled down his cheek. He immediately found some peace and was committed to help right the ship.

Embracing Your Crooked Rim

Visualizing the crooked rim from my childhood is a reflective practice I have used my entire career. Our thoughts shape our feelings. Our feelings shape our actions. We live our worldview through our thoughts, emotions, and behavior. When we feel bad, our thoughts and emotions may go to a negative place, which can produce negative impacts on our actions and behaviors. When we feel confident and positive, we can achieve peak performance.

We live our lives through our thoughts. If we want to advance a positive outlook on life and to increase our level of happiness, we must train and practice the way we think to achieve our desired outcomes. Each of us possesses the ability to access our own inner strength—our own resilience. Our mindset shapes and influences how we live in the moment and it frames our perception of and belief in what is possible. It shapes our overall performance physically, mentally, and emotionally. How we choose to show up every day for the game of life helps define who we are. And strengthening our resilience fuels our capacity to live life to the fullest.

The exercise that Cole implemented is called Appreciative Inquiry, a coaching strategy that works well to get yourself unstuck and to escape a slump. When I used this technique with my athletes, it was just called "coaching." My role and responsibility as a coach was to guide student-athletes so they could perform at their peak. Shifting to positive imagery and visualization transforms and raises our level of confidence, improves self-talk, minimizes doubt, and strengthens our emotional self-awareness. Perhaps surprisingly, optimism helps us get comfortable being *uncomfortable* as we embrace failure. When we approach failure with a net-forward, positive mindset, we can learn to fail with grace so failure does not become paralyzing or destructive. Failure becomes an opportunity to learn and to grow. Using this coaching strategy changes our mindset and gives individuals the ability to flip the switch back on and move forward.

* * *

We all have one or more crooked rim in our lives; the rims just look different for each of us. Our experiences, environment, and life-changing events produce mental and emotional obstacles and challenges that we can leverage to build resilience. Developing resilience in the barn yard, as I discovered, can be a game-changer later in life. You do not need a crooked rim nailed to a barn to get started. Start by mastering your mindset and choosing to never give up, to find a way, to fight, and to fail with no excuses—and commit to learn from your experiences and to transform them into motivators. Now, close your eyes and visualize your crooked rim. This is where your journey begins.

MASTER YOUR MINDSET: Your Crooked Rim

✦ What is your "Crooked Rim"?

✦ How can you apply the lessons learned from adversity to your life?

✦ What past peak performance(s) can you visualize when faced with adversity?

2

Road to the Final Four

"You get whatever accomplishment you are willing to declare."
—Georgia O'Keeffe—

Having big dreams, setting realistic goals and aspirations, overcoming obstacles, and experiencing breakthroughs are building blocks for resilience and well-being. Our journey in life creates a lifetime of memories and it also changes you. It did for me.

The Barn

"The Barn" at Williams Arena is the home of Golden Gopher basketball at the University of Minnesota. It is considered one of the greatest arenas in college basketball history. The entire state and alumni around the world love The Barn; every opponent hates it. With its elevated floor, intimate seating, and maroon and gold painted trim, it is one of the toughest places for opponents to play in the nation.

Early in my professional career, I declared to myself—and out loud to others—my long-term goals and my purpose in life. I was willing to do whatever it took to live it, taste it, and experience it to the fullest with the people who were the glue in my life. The journey is a process that binds the disparate parts of your life together, and I fell in love with the process.

My journey from a crooked rim nailed to a barn to The Barn at Williams Arena was tough, but when the going got tougher, so did I. The tougher the situation, the more resilient I became. There is more to resilience than simply avoiding mental and emotional challenges. Resilience represents an ability to cope with adversity and some do it much better than others. The overall goal of resilience is to thrive, personally and professionally.

Resilience is all about enduring the unexpected, overcoming it, and then learning how to recover from it. I learned a lot about unexpected situations and conditions between the four lines on The Barn's basketball court. Over time, I discovered that *you don't know what you don't know* and found that I was not 100 percent prepared to take on that big job until after I got in it. Now I realize that no one is ever 100 percent prepared but at 36 years old, when I was offered the opportunity to coach in the highly touted Big Ten conference, I embraced it and I had the confidence to dive in and do my best. Experience, success, and leadership ability put me in a position to get such a job; however, nothing ever prepared me completely until I actually sat in that chair.

Coaching big-time college basketball, particularly in The Barn, helped me master my mindset, strengthen my resilience, rewire my brain, and fortify my mental toughness. Two or three nights a week on game day, I stalked the sidelines doing my job in front of 14,625 people. Many of our games were on national television, which included CBS, Big Ten Network, ESPN, ESPN2, FOX Sports, and others. On national television, millions of people also watched me do my job, in real-time, from their couches. Across the raised floor sat every media outlet, beat writers, columnists, bloggers, and television reporters. Often on the other bench, a Hall of Fame coach would sit and strategize against me and my team.

Many former Minnesota Gopher greats' retired jerseys hung in the rafters. NCAA banners also were hanging as constant reminders of high expectations, every day and every game. We represented all who came before us and the ones who would come after. The Barn's hallowed environs inspired us and challenged us.

On game day, coaches and the athletes are on display while millions observe our performance, actions, and decision-making. In many ways, it feels like a virtual performance review in real time. And the people who observe your performance feel entitled to share their performance review immediately, shouting with cheers or jeers, or after the game online or on the radio or at the bar, stating their case about wanting you to stay or go. Resilience? Toughness? If you do not have either of them, you better develop them quickly.

On the raised floor of The Barn, I developed next-level resilience that I needed to confidently do my job publicly, through wins and losses, in good and bad times. It took daily situational training to strengthen and to sustain the level of success, to accept personal responsibility, and to own the expectations required of a Big Ten coach. Between the four lines, I not only strengthened my resilience, but I also learned to master my mindset. I thought I was already mentally tough, but the level of toughness that was needed for optimal peak performance mentally, emotionally, and spiritually at this level—and in this very public role—was much different. The ability to push past fatigue and exhaustion daily, year after year, and to learn how to reduce stress and burnout, to grow as a leader, and to build trust quickly, became the most important skills to strengthen as I pivoted into the business world.

When you focus on mastering your mindset, developing greater emotional strength, and enhancing trust, you are exercising and testing your Emotional Intelligence (EQ) muscles. In layman's terms, EQ encompasses the ability to be self-aware, to understand and to manage your own emotions, and to assess and to evaluate others' emotions—and then to customize your communications and actions to connect with others effectively. EQ is paramount to all relationships to build trust, whether player-coach, manager-employee, teammate-teammate, patient-doctor, etc. EQ training and practice should be part of all of us, in every profession and industry, and at all organizational levels. It is more than a single course or event we "must" attend; it represents a critical, ongoing life skill to enhance the growth and development of ourselves and those around us.

A high competency in EQ helps us improve our overall well-being, strengthen resilience, manage derailers, and develop leadership competencies that, in turn, will drive higher levels of productivity, mental health, trust, innovation, coaching skills, and authenticity. The quality of our relationships with others influences the degree of emotional resilience and trust for overall team and organizational effectiveness. The ability to master and maintain a high level of resilience paved the way for many trips to March Madness for my basketball teams.

March Madness

March Madness is one the best sporting events of the year. Millions fill out their brackets for the 2-week national championship tournament that falls into the perfect spot on the sporting calendar. On the first weekend, basketball games happen morning, noon, and night and we all expect "bracket buster" upsets and "Cinderella team" victories. Many fans root for the underdog—the team that may not be the most talented, but may be the toughest, bringing the fight and battling every night as a team. Teamwork and toughness, matchups, and a little luck thrown in are the key ingredients for Cinderella teams to pull off an upset during March Madness. College basketball's ultimate tournament is a one-and-done, survive-and-advance gauntlet that tests every team, player, and coach. The competition is built on resilience, mindset, momentum, frantic comebacks, and buzzer-beater shots. Most head coaches will never have the opportunity to experience the pinnacle of college basketball or ride the wave and coach a team all the way to the Final Four.

They say the Final Four—the tournament's penultimate three games that crown the champion—is where legends and hall-of-famers are born. The contenders step up and the rest go home. Moments of greatness often splash across our television screens when the best of the best embrace the moment. Over the entire NCAA tournament, and especially at the Final Four, journeys in life bring teammates and competitors together to create lasting memories and life-long relationships. This held true on the road to my Final Four moment in New Orleans.

Early in my life and throughout my coaching career, I committed to a set of core beliefs. My values always aligned with my beliefs; however, my values changed at different points in my life. The varying challenges and opportunities throughout our careers—at the start, in the middle, in a second career, and towards the end—change what we value most dearly. Early on, we may simply seek a good job and paycheck. As we progress in the working world, professional recognition and advancement may drive us. We may transform our careers, as I did when I left basketball coaching and entered the business coaching world, and find that we expect and desire greater fulfillment from our work. Toward the end of our careers, we may look for ways to leave a legacy, make a difference, and give back. You will experience different Final Four moments along this journey.

We all must strengthen our own resilience between our own four lines to determine what our own Final Four looks like in life, personally and professionally. Guiding my team to the Final Four and reaching the pinnacle of my coaching career was important to me and a highlight. I had big dreams and goals, I declared them out loud, and I learned to adapt, to be resourceful, and to brush myself off and continue moving forward when I fell down.

From Hardwood to Boardroom

My transition presented great opportunities to learn how coaching, team dynamics, and building championship cultures transferred from sports to business. It gave me a unique platform to help others develop high-performing teams and to explore how others might transition between industries, among organizational units, and at different organizational levels.

It was late spring, and I received a message through the LinkedIn networking platform from Renee, an attorney from Chicago. Renee was working with the Board Chair of a large non-profit in Chicago on strategic initiatives deemed critical to the organization's success. During their conversation, the Board Chair described major challenges they were having with Sally, the non-profit's CEO. The Chair expressed genuine concern that Sally's vision, priorities, and her leadership style were not a good fit for the organization. Relationships were fractured with many of the board members. Sally's leadership style was described as a "bull in a china shop" and she was making critical decisions without board approval. He asked Renee to identify a coach who could work with Sally and the board. It was pivotal that this coaching engagement work.

Sally had an incredible track record and reputation in Chicagoland as a change agent. She was successful in every position she had previously held in the corporate world. As a large non-profit organization, the board hired Sally to bring a different perspective, pace and strategy to the organization. So far, it was not working. They were not aligned or working well together. Renee asked about my immediate availability—they needed to see change quickly.

What I uncovered during the onboarding process, through many interviews and data gathering, was deep concern with deteriorating relationships. The top themes that stood out were lack of alignment with the board, disempowerment of her team, unilateral decision-making, and high turnover. Certainly, Sally's corporate experience could provide valuable perspectives in operating a successful non-profit, particularly one with significant scale. At the same time, her understanding of the unique leadership challenges faced by non-profits, and the ability to navigate relationships at the board and operational level, would be key to cross between the two worlds gracefully. If not, overall performance could be damaged very quickly.

Sally inherited her team and it was not the caliber she was told when she accepted the position. The former CEO had let many things slip over time and the culture needed rebuilding. Sally's intention was coming from a good place; she cared deeply about the purpose and the mission, and the value they brought to all stakeholders. Her actions and behaviors were less than what was expected to lead at this level and to work with the board. She adopted a passive and evasive leadership style out of stress and mistrust. While her heart was in the right place, Sally needed to figure out how to channel her expertise, passion, and energy in the right direction.

Like my Final Four team, Sally had to lean on all members of her team and her board to become a high-performing, value-creating unit. Sally learned to channel her drive, to initiate action effectively and collaboratively, and to adapt her approaches. Twelve months later, Sally experienced her own Final Four as the team bounced back and the organization thrived. As she implemented coaching strategies for building a resilient team and organization, Sally lifted morale and productivity to new heights.

At the Heart

My crooked rim experience influenced my resilience and my mindset every day. When I missed shots, I could have always blamed the rim. When we lost a game, I could have blamed others. My parents taught me that blaming others or making excuses did not build character, it only delayed the truth and led to disappointment in the long run. Whether on the court or in the office, competition and constraints test our character and values daily. If values are called into question or are compromised—operate with integrity, do the right thing, love your people, give of yourself, put others first, embrace the unknown—then it is time for you to go.

> *Developing coping and recovery mechanisms will help us manage disappointment throughout our lifetimes, but first, we must accept responsibility for our own role in failure.*

Personal accountability is key for building resilience, nurturing well-being, and reaching your own Final Four. We must recognize that our actions have an impact, and it is only through experiencing the impact first-hand that we learn to make better choices. Life is unpredictable and we will all experience setbacks and personal challenges in our lives. Developing coping and recovery mechanisms will help us manage disappointment throughout our lifetimes, but first, we must accept responsibility for our own role in failure.

We cannot always control what happens to us in life. However, we have total control over how we choose to respond to difficult situations. By taking personal responsibility for our reactions and our attitude, we will position ourselves to cope with and to manage our effort to achieve a desired outcome. If we want to reach our Final Four, personal accountability is critical. This value was ingrained in how I hired staff members, recruited players, and accepted responsibility for good and bad performance. As an imperative for my team, personal accountability embodied a non-negotiable expectation and became core behavior that drove our success. Developing a culture of accountability at all levels created a sense of team pride, ownership of results, and connection to our team brand.

The Night Before

On the night before our Elite Eight March Madness game against the Duke Blue Devils, there was incredible excitement, anxiety, and anticipation of a once-in-a-lifetime opportunity. We gathered the entire staff and players into my hotel suite for a team meeting. I can still remember this night like it was yesterday. We had built a resilient team and eliminated all outside distractions. Nothing would stand in our way and we had achieved our highest level mentally, emotionally, and purposefully. Our purpose was clear and we were going after it: win and earn a trip to our first Final Four.

Our journey earlier that season started out as a magical ride and the team was firing on all cylinders. In early February, the middle of the rugged Big Ten regular season, we were 15-0 and ranked 6th in the nation.

Then . . . IT HAPPENED. We were hit with a major setback. It was the middle of the Ohio State game on the road and everything was going our way. Out of the timeout, Lindsay went away from the play, she drove full speed down the middle of the lane, and she ran into one of her teammates. She went crashing to the floor. Everyone's hearts dropped and our perfect season flashed through everyone's minds. Instantly, fear and uncertainty rushed in as we circled up and took care of Lindsay and each other.

Lindsay broke two bones in her wrist and was out for five weeks. Her injury threatened to torpedo the season and our vision of the Final Four. It left us asking, *Why in the world would this happen now? Why would it happen to our All-American, our leader, our point guard . . . Lindsay Whalen?*

As a coach, you start looking at the schedule and counting the games. How many games do we have left? How will this affect our momentum and team dynamics, our record, our national ranking, our NCAA tournament seed, and our NCAA tournament chances? From the beginning, our hope, dreams, and vision were the Final Four. Now what? Life does not always work out according to the plan and our resilience would be tested like never before.

We faced a lot of adversity over the next eight games, in what seemed like a very long stretch. The obstacles, roadblocks, and the tension each game brought to my staff and team became unbearable at times. After one game during this strength, we sat down as a team and had a heart-to-heart team meeting. As their coach, I wanted to make sure I communicated how much I believed in them and how proud I was of their resilience, of not giving up or making excuses. Instead, they did what winners do. They worked harder, their preparation was seamless, and our resilience peaked. The team trusted each other and committed to figuring it out together. We stayed the course, took blows like champs, embraced every roadblock, and pivoted each game.

We hoped it would be enough to get an NCAA tournament bid and we would get Lindsay back on the floor and on point. Playing the final stretch without our star player—who led the team in every statistical and intangible category—took perseverance and mental toughness. Instead of giving in and losing our momentum, the entire team got better, more confident, and more connected. During that stretch, everyone took on new roles, accepted greater responsibilities, shifted strategy overnight, and communicated transparently to build deeper trust. We all were "learning on the job." We battened down the hatches and personal accountability became the glue for our team. We never wavered and we did not lower the bar. We just believed.

Big Moments

Our team's culture bred confidence, supported risk taking, and emphasized learning to fail with grace. Our players and coaches learned that pressure was a privilege and an opportunity to improve—like iron sharpening iron.

Lindsay and the doctors decided that her first game back would be in the first round of the NCAA tournament, a matchup against UCLA at The Barn. She practiced only one day before our open practice to the public in the NCAA tournament. She did not take a shot for over a month because she had broken her right wrist, her shooting hand. At practice, 800 people showed up with anticipation to watch the team. Lindsay took her first shot in five weeks, everyone took a deep breath with eyes as big as saucers, and we all watched the flight of the ball . . . SWISH. Straight through the basket, nothing but net! The stands exploded, and we all just looked at each other with big smiles and relief. We were ready.

The evening before facing Duke, we had our regular team meeting the night before the game. Everyone stood in a circle in my hotel suite as my assistant pulled out a plastic bag with 20 pair of scissors wrapped in individual packages. Everyone held out their hands and closed their eyes. We listened closely and took 10 deep breaths. My assistant asked us to imagine that we were on an elevator on the tenth floor. We were asked to count down slowly as we traveled down the elevator to the first floor. He said, visualize yourself with the person next to you celebrating after the buzzer sounds, climbing up the ladder, and then cutting down the net. He passed out a pair of scissors to each one of us and asked that we write on the package what it would mean to win and for whom we would play.

Everyone took a few minutes to reflect, mindful and grateful for the opportunity we had in front of us. Tears rolled down many cheeks and we felt the power of giving ourselves permission to be vulnerable in the moment. We all knew the battle we conquered to get to this moment and to enjoy this opportunity. The scissors then were collected and packed into the plastic bag. Our final words to the team that evening was powerful: when the final buzzer sounds tomorrow night, you will cut down the net with your own scissors. After taking down Duke the next night, that is exactly what we did.

We beat Duke, 82-75, for our fourth straight March Madness win and a spot in the Final Four. When the final buzzer sounded, two-time all-American Janel McCarville carried me off the court. I looked up and saw that Janel was headed to the Gatorade cooler. Whatever happened during the season, just like the final seconds of the game, was not what we had drawn up. We had reached our dream and how we got there was not how we had planned . . . but we were headed to the Final Four.

Define and Decide

Every moment when we were coaching, teaching, motivating, inspiring, and practicing positive psychology, we were preparing for our ideal peak performance. We experienced mindfulness, presence, visualization and gratitude as we reached our Final Four milestone with the most important people in our lives. There were so many life lessons learned during that eight-month journey. It was not just the end result that mattered, it was the process. The adversity, daily setbacks, negative thoughts, mental fortitude, injuries, struggles, and failure set us up for success.

* * *

While our team's trip to the Final Four was a unique opportunity, we are not limited to experiencing just one Final Four moment in our lives. A Final Four could be something small or huge, and we could have personal and professional versions. We define what it looks like and feels like. No matter what Final Four(s) you strive to accomplish, taking time along the way to be present and to develop a high level of self-awareness as it provides the foundation for our resilience and mental health.

As a coach, it is rewarding when a client defines and experiences her own Final Four. I am excited to help you realize yours in your life. Declare your desired accomplishment. Then, believe and you will be on your way. And when you get to that Final Four, remember to cut down the net to celebrate!

MASTER YOUR MINDSET: Your Road to the Final Four

✦ What Final Four(s) have you achieved? What new Final Four(s) are you striving toward?

✦ What negative self-talk will you have to change to Master Your Mindset?

✦ How can you improve your Emotional Intelligence?

3

The Transition

"We plant seeds of resilience in the ways
we process negative events."
–SHERYL SANDBERG–

I was at the top of my game when I decided to change careers. I remember thinking that people do it all the time—for different reasons and in different ways. In my case, I was fired after a long and successful career coaching college basketball. After my firing, I stepped away from the sport, abandoning a professional identity, and left a known legacy with no clear understanding of what my future might hold or what my sense of self might be.

The Final Buzzer

We all experience final buzzers at various points in our lives—a sudden ending followed by an immediate transition—and some people encounter them more often than others. Sometimes, the buzzer sounds at the end of a victory and sets a desirable progression to "what's next" in motion. Other times, the buzzer sounds with the shock of a defeat and the suddenness of departure or emptiness of loss.

Overnight, what was written on my name tag, how I introduced myself, and how others identified with me changed. Everyone, not just people who have been fired or fear they are about to be, must continuously pivot their skillsets. I was in my late forties and decided it was worth undertaking a major change because I knew I had enough time for a rewarding second career.

Life transitions can sound and feel like a final buzzer. In sports, it could be a freshman arriving for a first day of training camp after leaving high school and home, the final game celebrating senior day, a career-ending injury, mental health challenges, drug or alcohol addiction, or coaching your last game and leaving a legacy behind. *How many life transitions have you experienced or are expecting?* Being able to envision and to prepare for your next chapter is not just good defense, it is great offense.

In life, we experience transition in many ways. It is important to discover want we want our next chapter to look like, what it means, and how we want to live. We transition into new jobs, lose loved ones, become an empty nester, divorce, lose a job, change careers, retire, get new leadership, and experience new roles. Relocating to a new city, starting a new relationship, and finding a new doctor, dentist, therapist, or even a new hair stylist are all part of transitions.

During our transitions, it is important to find purpose, hope, focus, and a sense of self. If you plan to remain in the workforce long enough to reach your financial goals, you must continually pivot and evolve professionally to find a new context for work and to develop new skills. As you transition, make sure you "get with the times". Not being on social media is no longer optional, especially for executives and leaders; we need to have a positive brand presence to demonstrate that you are staying current professionally. Even the basic notion of writing a résumé is antiquated; your résumé is LinkedIn . . . and Google.

> *Being able to envision and to prepare*
> *for your next chapter in life is not just good*
> *defense, it is great offense.*

These prototypical final buzzers can test our resilience tremendously. And to further complicate things, each of us must contend with an internal narrator: a voice that provides a constant running commentary of our lives. It is almost as if we are "live on air" with our own color commentator who anticipates, observes, and critiques our every move. This inner play-by-play might even project what our emotions and actions might be. *Have you been listening to your inner voice lately? What is it saying to you about your final buzzer or next chapter?* You're not alone. Human beings all have the mental software programmed to be our biggest cheerleader and biggest critic. The context and content of our narration depends on what program we open in the computer of our mind. Fortunately, we fill the position of our own Chief Narrative Officer responsible for our own internal dialogue.

The dark side of transition often associates change with fear, uncertainty, doubt, and the unknown. On the brighter side, transition or change can enable us to develop a high level of optimism. Mastering our mindset around how we embrace transition and respond to the final buzzer can be exciting. We may be full of anticipation, ready to explore new possibilities and take steps to live a more fulfilling life. Still, we must contend with external conditions as we bolster our optimism—like economic downturns, social upheaval, or health pandemics that darken the global psyche. Stress, fear, anxiety, uncertainty, and limiting beliefs dominate our minds and conversations. Strengthening and re-imagining our resilience and how we handle these times are critical for our overall resilience, well-being, and mental health.

Final buzzers do not just signal an ending; they ring in a new beginning. When my final buzzer sounded at the time of my firing, I swirled from the known to the unknown, from comfortable to uncomfortable, and from what was to what will be. My sense of self and security had been rocked and I was lost, grieving, fearful, anxious, and uncertain. I experienced withdrawal from a demanding and consuming job and psychological stress that challenged my resilience and well-being.

The Pivot

When I transitioned into my second career, I applied caution to my words and script. I was not "reinventing" who I am; I was "pivoting" my transferrable skills developed over 27 years to a new arena: the business world. During my transition I experienced loss, loneliness, grief, uncertainty, and the unknown. And, I had to overcome an "addiction" to the annual recruiting-training-competition cycle and all the ups and downs that accompanied it. I had to master my mindset to shift my perspective, learning how to flip my story and its plot upside down and accept the difficulties as positives, challenges, competitiveness, and expanded growth opportunities. Leveraging the power of positivity and vulnerability has always been a game changer for me professionally, and now it was being called upon like a full court press.

In my decades of front-line experience as a coach, I deployed positive psychology as a coaching method every day with my staff and players. It became innate and crucial for motivating, inspiring, and getting the best out of people and teams. Now, during my second career, I recognized the importance of certifications in positive psychology and well-being to master these strategies I used with elite athletes then and with clients today. In everything I signed up for, I wanted to be the best and to deliver the best coaching and training to the individuals with whom I work. With high expectations for myself, I set the bar higher than ever before.

> *Leveraging the power of positivity and vulnerability was a game changer for me professionally, and in my transition from the court to the business world I called upon it like a full court press.*

People call and email every day and ask, *What did you do, why did you start a second career, and how did you know what you wanted to do?* And of course, the most frequently asked question: *How did you have the confidence to do something other than coach college basketball?* Many people are afraid because they think all they know is where they are now. Many people say they cannot lose their job or leave their position because they are afraid of what's next. The mindset of fear creates a crisis of confidence limiting the ability to reach new horizons and flourish. In reality, they should believe they can do anything to which they set their minds.

Mastering Your Mindset

Mastering your mindset is the first step to embrace the final buzzer and to initiate a life transition. This is natural in sports.

Athletes train their bodies, minds, souls, and spirits every day in order to compete at a high level successfully. Retraining the mind is a step that cannot be skipped. Thriving through transition depends on managing the inner dialogue.

Final buzzers bring an end to one phase and introduce a new beginning. They close the book to one chapter and we pivot our skills that we have mastered our entire lives, transferring them to the next chapter. Experiencing my final buzzer taught me that I was not reinventing myself as a coach or person; I was pivoting the skills I had already developed and mastered to the next opportunity. The current of life presents unpredictability like a whitewater rafting trip, running through rushing rapids, stalling in calm eddies, getting sucked into swirling holes, and navigating rocks and fallen trees. Recognizing that life is a journey, I focused on the only option for me: I would keep growing, grinding, competing, and moving toward life's goals.

Developing Self-Awareness

What would happen if everything you worked for your entire life was taken away or you decided to walk away? You would be tested mentally and emotionally like never before, like I was after my firing. My overall record as a collegiate head coach tallied 305 wins and an overall Big Ten mark of 104-94. After finishing my final season with a record of 22-13, my final buzzer sounded. It told me 27 years of experience, an NCAA Final Four, numerous NCAA tournament appearances, the highest graduation rates, and more wins than any coach in program history were not enough. I was highly respected in the game, on campus and in the business community over the previous 12 years, yet I felt stripped of my sense of self and my identity overnight.

I had no idea how difficult the transition would be. I started by defining my values, strengths, purpose, and meaning and the vision I wanted for the rest of my life. After going through this process, pivoting my skillset seemed seamless. Still, the Chief Narrative Officer sometimes showed up in my head. I could see the crooked rim and the four lines in the barn in my rearview mirror. This is where my resilience and mental toughness were honed and tested daily for decades. This would be the foundation from which to launch into my next level.

While I was pivoting, I envisioned and defined how my next Final Four moment would look. My new Final Four would not include loss and endings, but the embrace of new beginnings. Recovering from the stark reality of the buzzer, I picked myself up, dusted myself off, and continued the journey of learning new skills, gaining new knowledge, and shifting my mindset to embrace all possibilities. As Ringo Starr sang, written by George Harrison, "It don't come easy". My transition was a process that challenged all four of the core competencies: physical, mental, emotional, and spiritual. I was prepared to enter into a new season of life in this major transition, leveraging skills key to my physical health, emotional well-being, and mental health.

It only took me a few months to choose my next path, and immediately it seemed right for my life. I would transition from the sports world to the business world as a leadership coach and start my own consulting firm. As this vision took shape, I found peace and direction, further developing increased self-awareness. I felt a flip switch in my mind and heart; I was ready and excited to build another legacy. We all have this ability. Successfully managing a difficult transition takes mindfulness, self-awareness, and intentionality to conquer the unexpected.

> *Successfully managing a difficult transition takes mindfulness, self-awareness, and intentionality to conquer the unexpected.*

By simply pivoting my skills, I could still do what I loved: coaching people and teams and enabling high performance. I had more to give and more people to impact, just in a different arena. This shift and focus would further sharpen my mindset and self-awareness as I built out my new path forward. And, it gave me the perspective I needed to help others face tough transitions. Here is how I helped one of my client's transition and pivot his skillset in a similar scenario.

CEO Transition

I was referred to Dave, a seasoned and successful CEO who owned a multi-million-dollar business. Referrals are most of my business. In the sports world, the best athletes want to work with the best coaches, play for the best teams and organizations, and have the best teammates around them. The best flourish when they are around like-minded, driven, and successful people. After my transition, I was only four short years ahead of Dave.

Dave sold a business that consisted of 14 offices across the Midwest and East Coast. He was transitioning from being the CEO and owner of one of the most successful healthcare practices in the country. The burnout, stress, industry changes, competition, people challenges, and constant demands were a daily grind and he was tired of putting fires out daily. Dave had other passions and business interests and wanted the time to explore innovation for his industry.

The healthcare industry was changing rapidly and he wanted to pursue other passions for which his company left no time.

These passions were not hunting, fishing, or golf. His interests were growing the business, driving innovation, and giving back. He also wanted to travel around the world speaking, teach classes at a university, develop new products, write a book, and start another business or two. Innovation stood apart as one of his key interests and strengths. As he put out fires and managed his company, he lacked the time to think about the future of technology with telemedicine, or how virtual reality and artificial intelligence might elevate his industry.

Dave was brilliant and an industry leader in his field. He saw me from afar transition from a career that was all-consuming and high octane. He needed accountability, direction, and a roadmap at this stage of his life. Dave expressed a desire to dial back and to learn to let go of the grind. Such a shift would require a change in mindset and great self-awareness of his values and priorities at this stage of his life.

As I mentioned, Dave observed my transition from afar. He knew that transitioning from the sports world to the business world took courage and he was ready to do the same. His goal was to reach the pinnacle of his profession, his Final Four. Drive, work ethic, resilience, and purpose to impact others were ingrained and a shared lifestyle for both of us. Dave had traveled a lot, worked late nights, and sacrificed his personal life to get to this point. He was now ready to pivot the love and joy of his work into the next chapter, something else just as fulfilling. He wanted a coach and thought partner who had sat in his chair and already travelled down this path. The journey with a coach who would support, challenge, and understand the struggle was exactly what both of us needed. We were on this journey together; I was just a little further down the path.

Transitioning to the corporate world as a leadership consultant and thought leader would require more than X's and O's and a pair of sweatpants. How would my experience with the crooked rim and the barn pivot to the boardroom? Finding meaning and purpose in serving others may be done with a ball or hockey stick, in a pool or on a track, or with a stethoscope, scalpel, or even a badge. Every skill we develop in our lifetimes are transferable and can help us pivot to what's next.

I refined my resilience model and shaped my understanding of individual and team resilience through the knowledge, skills, and experience I cultivated in the sports world; navigating my own transition and transformation; and achieving certifications in executive coaching, emotional intelligence, resilience, health and wellness coaching through the national board of medical examiners, and global team coaching. I was ready to guide and lead others facing what I had experienced. Living through my own transition was transformational and being alongside Dave was rewarding.

The Struggle

I have never shared my struggles publicly about my transition from the world of college athletics, a familiar lifestyle that had consumed my entire life. I was sure I felt what professional athletes face when they stop playing the game and their next chapter awaits. During times of crisis, unrest, and uncertainty, resilience becomes a capability we all must master. My spouse, Lynn, watched me struggle, navigate, grow, struggle again, and then sky-rocket—often feeling and hurting as much if not more as you face difficulties.

My entire life I was on a hamster wheel and, suddenly, the wheel stopped. Almost two years after I left college athletics, and I was still addicted to the pace, intensity, and "being on" constantly.

I was addicted to the stress, the pressure, the expectations, the responsibility, and the drive to win. We all have addictions we must face during a transition, such as the intensity I experienced or simply familiarity and predictability of the status quo. For me, the struggle involved coming down and letting it go, learning to slow down and relax, asking for help, taking a day and weekends off, enjoying the holidays for the first time in my professional life, and appreciating the quiet once there were no more daily fires to put out. Coaches have an addiction to the rush, the spotlight, the power, the celebrity status, and the rewards and success. It is all we know and it was an intense lifestyle. During this period, I realized I had to commit to adjust my wiring and to find a new normal.

My client Dave also found that he needed to rewire and to retrain his mind, choices, and passion. His new trajectory involved pivoting his skillset to telemedicine, virtual reality, and artificial intelligence. While the pandemic ravaged global health, Dave's vision became a reality and the health crisis presented opportunities for him to soar again in his new businesses. His values also shifted, and he learned to carve out time to attend his son's lacrosse games on weekends and his daughter's dance competitions. He learned how to take weekends off and to enjoy getaway weekends with his wife to their favorite spa and resort. Instead of stress and strain, Dave now looks forward to peace and possibility—just like I do.

* * *

While transitioning and pivoting our skills can present one of the most difficult challenges in our life, it can also be one of the most enriching. Dave and I did not waste any time. Like the pace of our careers, we appreciated speed, high octane, and winning. Most people are afraid to transition or to experience their final buzzer because of the fear of the unknown. Mastering our mindset, cultivating resilience, and developing a high level of self-awareness gives us the confidence and belief that we all can pivot in life and as leaders.

MASTER YOUR MINDSET: Your Transition

✦ What life transitions have you experienced (or are expecting) and how have you managed them?

✦ When your inner narrator provides negative or critical commentary, how do you shut it down and move forward?

✦ What skills and passions do you possess that are transferrable to other opportunities if you seek to—or are forced to—transition?

4

Destined for More

"Look closely at the present you're constructing;
it should look like the future you're dreaming."
—ASHLEY WALKER—

A Chinese proverb says that a journey of a thousand miles begins with a single step. My transformative journey from the court to the board room looked like a horizon a thousand miles in the distance. And when I began to move forward, the first step required a significant mental shift, not a physical step. So, I took the first tentative but exciting step.

The First Step

My first step to transformation involved preparing for a world that did not exist in my mind. I had no framework to understand the business world and how it differed from big-time collegiate athletics. Eventually I would discover many similarities, but out of the gate the change from my predictable environment and comfortable structure was dramatic. The reality of life is that we should be changing, adapting, exploring, and running toward obstacles constantly. We all can cultivate a resilient mindset to embrace change. With the right mindset and belief, we can abandon fear and resistance and experience many "aha moments" in our lives.

My transition from the sports world to the business world, eventually building a successful consulting firm, started as just a wild dream. I needed to broaden my world view and expand and deepen my knowledge in ways that we all should strive for and experience. If I ever decided to go back to coaching college basketball, which I had (and have) no intention to do, it would be a very different experience. There is a big difference between the role of a sports coach and a leadership coach. As a college basketball coach, I made every decision, answered everyone's questions, and solved all of the problems as the program's "CEO".

While players and assistant coaches look to you for direction and await your directives and instruction, coaching clients today requires a transformative shift to alter my operating structure intellectually, emotionally, and physically. Successful and effective coaches provide a framework, strategies, and knowledge that inspire and enable clients to find solutions. Changing my operating structure further strengthened my courage, confidence, well-being, and growth. Once I made the front pivot, there was no turning back. I had made many sacrifices personally and professionally—like all athletes, coaches, and business people—but this change involved growth, not sacrifice.

My mindset never wavered throughout every stage of my sports-to-business transition. Continuing to motivate, impact, and inspire others as I had done for nearly 30 years heightened my awareness of the importance of my goals and the value I would bring to all stakeholders. Leading with purpose has always been my "why" and my professional pivot reminded me of it often. My transition continues today, and the process has raised my game to a higher level of leadership. I bet yours has been (or will be), too.

In the Zone

Players and coaches all know what it feels like to be "in the zone". Your greatest shooters feel a "heat check" on the court when they pull up from deep and they know they will hit the shot. Players feel that the basket is as big as an ocean, and when you feel it, everyone can see success coming from the sidelines and in the stands. It is like floating down the river with the current in a state of supreme focus, like being in a "state of flow." After great performances, athletes can describe the heightened feeling of awareness and performance. "In the zone" or "flow" state you feel invincible, as if the game slowed down, the crowd noise fell silent, and you focused on the goal singularly. You have complete control over your own movements and actions without concern of your competition.

Mihaly Csikszentmihalyi was one of my teachers as I worked to secure my certification in positive psychology and well-being. He developed a comprehensive theory around a "state of flow" concept and not only applied it to sports, but to work, life, education, music, and purpose. This did not seem like a new concept to me; I lived in a world where being in the zone or flow was a practice that coaches teach to their athletes, as it is needed to perform at your peak every day. Getting on a roll, having momentum, and performing at our peak potential was expected in sports. If not, "we need to make a change in leadership" or "I need to find another player who can get the job done".

Coaches are expected to develop their athletes and teams to perform at their peak potential every day, year after year. Training and developing their minds to fully connect with a goal creates the conditions required to find the zone and flow. After considering this process and strategy athletically, I learned to convert the method to focus with clients on their optimal performance. Once clients find their zone, they feel a transformation to perform at their best, just like the shooter who cannot miss a shot.

> *When you develop the ability to see everything "off the ball", you develop an intuitive sense, have your finger on the pulse, and become a strategic thinker.*

As the head coach, my role always was to see the bigger picture, set strategy, and define the purpose and vision for the program. I had the ability to see the whole game, the panoramic view. Many novice coaches, players, fans—and business leaders—follow and only see the ball. When you only watch the ball, you miss what is developing and happening around you. "Ball watching" is like narrowly focusing on day-to-day operations or quarter to quarter, as the task master plods along and crosses tasks off the list, while seeing only what is in front of them and thinking tactically. When you develop the ability to see everything "off the ball" and from the "top of the stadium", you develop an intuitive sense, have your finger on the pulse, and become a strategic thinker for a long-term vision. *When you step onto your "court", are you two or three steps ahead of the play and can you see the complete game and the bigger picture?*

The game slows down when we push ourselves to think beyond the ball and we put in the work to evolve to the next level. Through my transformation, I lifted my game and steadily strengthened my resilience and mental toughness. In athletics, I had big dreams and goals; I still do and as a seasoned executive I have learned to appreciate the importance of slowing the game down at this juncture in my life. As all-time hockey great and now NHL and Olympic team executive Wayne Gretzky said, "Skate to where the puck is going, not where it has been." Look forward, not behind, and anticipate what is required to get to the next level.

Leader as Coach

Coaching represents a key skill for front-line managers and beyond. When leaders are great coaches, everyone wins—individual, team, and the organization. Coaching is integral to develop a culture of learning at all levels of the organization. Success does not happen in isolation; as coaches, leaders motivate and inspire others to perform at their best as a team.

We all start our careers developing "competency-based" expertise, knowledge, and skills. As we matured, we were expected to have all the right answers, ideas, and solutions. Many managers and organizations continue to lead with a 20th Century "competency-based" mindset and approach. Does this sound familiar? When leaders pursue this level of need and control, they limit their own growth and development as well as those on the team. Leaders must transform into coaches; the process and journey create limitless opportunities for everyone.

During my progression into a Big Ten head coach, I developed into a leader and then, eventually, a true coach. This transformation benefited me and my players, but more importantly, set an example and expectation for my staff. True coaching creates an ongoing culture of learning practiced daily. When leaders become coaches, people become more confident and motivated, which leads to higher performance, productivity, and retention. They build relationships of trust that will lift others to the next level consistently.

Organizations with strong coaching cultures transform their people and organizations from a competency-based emphasis to a possibility-based focus. In a coaching culture, everyone builds resilience and experiences opportunities to reach their own Final Fours. Leaders who build coaching skills will have the ability to perform at a higher level. They show up with vision and motivation, enabling them to make different choices and decisions that impact growth and develop a stronger bench.

Our transitions present the opportunity to transform our lives, positively and negatively. Some people live life never facing the kind of adversity that others do. While a blessing to avoid extreme adversity, such individuals may never know how these life circumstances shape and build resilience. Still others experience life as one gut-wrenching rollercoaster rise and drop after another, facing adversity at every turn. In the end, we choose how we perceive and define the challenges, obstacles, and potholes of life—are they insurmountable or just another mile in the marathon of life? Overcoming stress, fear, anxiety, or a lack of confidence requires a commitment to strengthen resilience.

If your organization does not measure or assess your ability to coach and to develop others, that will likely change soon. Today, organizations are evolving to performance- and strategy-focused cultures and expecting their leaders to coach in real-time and to give feedback on the spot. This is vital for developing talent, meeting performance goals, and planning for advancement and succession. Many leaders are held accountable for their own performance as well as team performance management and development, with an objective to build high-performing teams. Unfortunately, most leaders are never taught why or how! My coaching and developing of leaders over the past few years emphasizes the purpose and the tools to build high-performing teams. Transforming leaders into true coaches will draw energy, motivation, creativity, and learning out of your people. If coaching skills represent a gap in your toolkit, get started today.

Searching for Balance

As I integrated research on resilience with typical patterns of thinking, it provided a clear roadmap for my own transformation and my path in coaching others. We make unconscious assessments, and our Chief Narrative Officer runs thoughts through our minds about ourselves and our outlooks on life. Some thoughts are accurate and some are not.

The global health crisis and today's world offer a real-time example. For many, just surviving today requires more than just hope—it demands a shift in mindset, thinking, and actions. To truly live life limitlessly, specific attributes and competencies are required and must be practiced each day so they become habits that change our lives. *On a scale of one to ten, what is your level of resilience today?*

My level of resilience floated up and down for the first two years of my transition. I was addicted to the intensity of coaching for so many years, and I did not fully appreciate what mental, emotional, and physical effects it had until the madness stopped. The rush that comes with preparing for and winning games, the frenetic pace of the season, and the grind of landing new players and blue-chip recruits became a craving, an urgent need. Having the Big Ten platform, the prestige of the Head Coach title, and the celebrity status and trappings that accompanied the position, I felt very uncomfortable knowing what I would be missing and I was uncertain how I would replace the intensity.

> *For many, just surviving today requires*
> *more than just hope—it demands a shift in*
> *mindset, thinking, and actions.*

During the first two years of my transition, the calendar year caused cravings and emotional mood swings around holiday tournaments, the start of school, the Big Ten season, March Madness, and the July recruiting calendar (which is one part I do not miss!). The romance of March Madness, mixed with the anticipation of National Signing Day for high school recruits, had me trapped on an emotional roller-coaster. I was living in an unconscious, intuitive burnout and plagued by loss, burnout, grief, and loneliness. At the same time, I was excited to get my life back. I could slowly feel the transformation taking hold so I kept moving forward.

Flipping Your Script

Life offers turning points, or inflection points, when we find the inspiration and motivation to move forward and to rewrite our own unique story. My transition and subsequent transformation resulted directly from "flipping my script" in my own mind and confidently communicating it to others. I was trying to write the script and be the actor, the producer, and my own critic. I was not broken and did not need to "reinvent" myself; I simply needed to pivot my skillset and use it to fulfill my life-long purpose: to coach others to their peak performance. I leveraged my self-regard, optimism, work ethic, human skills, and the ability to motivate around a shared purpose as I wrote the new chapter in my own story. Flipping my script, in my mind, gave me the confidence to move forward to accomplish my next Final Four moment(s).

I have been privileged to work with many phenomenal individuals. One client, Chip, was a high performer and on his second stint as Chief of Police after "retiring" from his previous Chief post. He already qualified for his pension and found that he was too driven and in his prime to retire officially. In his mid-forties, he led one of the largest law enforcement departments and at one of the most prestigious institutions in the country. At the same time, he found himself at a juncture in life wanting to be present at home in his family's lives.

As the Chief of Police, Chip worked 12 to 14 hours a day, seven days a week. I became Chip's senior executive coach during this time and was a resource in the right place at the right time. He needed support, a thought partner, and someone who had just made similarly pivotal decisions, choices, and transitions in their life. Leaving a "big job", a position of power, and a powerful identity was not an easy script to flip for me, just as flipping his own script would present Chip with challenges. At a pivotal point in his life, I supported Chip as he made the decision to step away, to take a "less prestigious" role, and to find peace at last.

Chip had already notched several Final Four moments in reaching the pinnacle of his career. He spent a considerable amount of time reflecting and introspectively evaluating his values, thoughts, and emotions at this point in his life. These decisions are never easy and the transition journey is difficult. With an ability to master your mindset, you begin to realize that you are transforming to another level, personally and professionally. As he sorted through and clarified his mindset, Chip and I laughed a lot and compared war stories about the crucible and intensity of our leadership experiences. I joked with him that working seven days a week and 12 to 14 hours a day did not sound like a retirement job. In the end, with my support, he gave himself permission to do what was right at this point in his life.

The Power Within

Transitions are daunting, whether for a first responder and police commissioner of 30 years, for a CEO let go after 5 years, for a fired head coach currently transitioning to an assistant coach role and moving across the country, or for a successful military Captain with six deployments to Afghanistan and Iraq now in a civilian role. I am proud to have a role in their success stories; however, all transitions are not home runs. Many individuals cannot move on and let go of the past, transfer their skillsets, ask for help, manage discomfort, accept fear of failure, and embrace the unknown. Pivoting is an opportunity for success that takes resilience and toughness—and success is not earned easily.

I have experienced several transformations throughout my career and did not recognize the impact on my life until years later. Being brave, courageous, driven, visionary, resilient, and optimistic are required skills to develop on this journey. If you are able to take a step backwards, in order to take two steps forward, your growth mindset can help prevent sabotaging your health and happiness. What we learn is that power lies within and is not what is perceived from others externally. Being able to stretch yourself, add new skills, and identify a support system fuels limitless opportunities. Whether you choose or are forced into transition, embrace it, see it as an opportunity, and know that it will make you stronger along the way.

> *Whether you choose or are forced into transition, embrace it, see it as an opportunity, and know that it will make you stronger along the way.*

Police Chief Chip flipped his script and developed a transparent and heartfelt message to capture his vision. Many call it a personal vision statement; however you define it, a stated commitment serves as an anchor through unforeseen turbulence. With your purpose and vision clarified, the transformation then can fully utilize your strengths and self-awareness, enabling you to take inventory and learn new skills and behaviors to fill gaps. Most of my life, I have instilled confidence, belief, and hope in others—but first I had to do it for myself. My crooked rim experience constructed the foundation and then I mastered it between the four lines of the basketball court. Chip found peace because it was inside of him the whole time; he just needed to marshal his confidence, belief, and hope. I know peace and success are inside of you, too!

Inside-Out Mindfulness

Growing up on the Ohio farm, I was naturally attracted to the outdoors. Observing nature and wildlife, climbing trees, riding dirt bikes, hiding away in my treehouse, and snowmobiling and boating were part of my childhood. I have carried these experiences through adulthood and keep them top of mind during my transformation. Like these experiences, exercising daily continues as a core element of my own mental wellness, health, and well-being.

During a recent business trip, I went on an early morning run before delivering a keynote speech. The weather was perfect, a crisp 52 degrees, the sky was powder blue and I could hear the birds chirping. The air smelled of cut grass, jasmine flowers, and fresh mulch. The neighborhood was flush with an array of flowers and bright colors that reminded me of Mom's garden on the farm. I felt at home, my spirit was uplifted, and the feeling of gratitude made me smile as I picked up the pace.

Two young deer stood about 20 yards ahead, nibbling grass, crab apples, and shrubs. Their tanned, spotted coats glimmered richly in the sun. Judging from their size and color, I assumed they were three to four months old, judging from seeing them in our fields and woods on the farm. Here I was in the middle of a residential neighborhood with a large conference center not too far away, and it was amazing how still they stayed as I jogged by. I turned to take one more look before heading back to the hotel to get ready for my presentation. Feeling the fresh air and seeing nature filled my bucket for the remainder of the day.

As I caught my breath and wiped my face with my t-shirt, I was already starting to get in the zone for my keynote. Being in nature and even viewing scenes of nature reduces anger, fear, and stress, and increases positive feelings. Exposure to nature not only makes us feel better emotionally, but it also contributes to our physical well-being, reducing blood pressure, heart rate, muscle tension, and the production of stress hormones. As a national-board certified health and wellness coach, through the national board of medical examiners, learning this added science and data to the sense of comfort I always felt in nature. That day, as one of only 5,000 certified health and wellness coaches globally, I was fired up to speak to a full house on resilience, the most needed leadership skill and most compelling topic in the world.

Still cooling down, I walked outside to the bistro to relax with coffee, a piece of fruit, and yogurt. I had a pre-game routine and it was game time today. Developing routines in our life increases our confidence level; before a "game", my routine consists of a run, light snack, and coffee, and includes taking a moment for mindfulness and focus. As I sipped my coffee, I flashed back to the pre-game talks when I encouraged my players to play hard and to have fun and I reminded them of their readiness for the moment. I grabbed a pad of paper and pen from the hotel lobby and quickly wrote down four reminders: mindset, self-awareness, confidence, and optimism. I walked briskly to my room with renewed energy and with excitement to deliver my best keynote yet.

My run confirmed my belief that over time, as we expand our self-awareness, acquire new skills, implement new practices, and lean on past experiences, "mental muscle memory" develops through conscious effort and consistency. We increase our levels of resilience by learning to adapt, embracing a growth mindset, and believing in limitless possibilities. My mental muscle memory kicked in and I was feeling boundless energy and passion, ready to engage with the audience, my team for the day.

Reframing our transitions gains power when we leverage resilience and build mental strength. My practice of mindfulness produces benefits in many ways in my life and was pivotal in my transition from sports to business. This mental practice allows me to focus on my development from the inside-out. Mindfulness is for everyone, especially during crooked rim times of crisis characterized by uncertainty, stress, fear, anxiety, and trauma.

You can integrate daily mindfulness practice and training into your life. It took me a few years to learn how to relax, slow down, be patient, and develop the mental skills I needed for success today. I practice mindfulness several different ways and it has impacted me holistically, from exercising by running or Bikram yoga to calm my mind, creating a quiet space for silent reflection (e.g., walking my dogs, shutting out external noise, and eliminating distractions), and just taking time to think and breathe. Once mindfulness became a habit, and I was more comfortable with the "discomfort" of silence, I knew how significant it would be for other senior level leaders and high performers, and also during and after their transitions. Like high-performing athletes, corporate athletes need training to instill new skills to help them find their peak performance state. Mindfulness serves as a cornerstone in the foundation of a leader's skillset.

* * *

I am confident that you can activate similar capabilities, mastering your mindset and leaning into mindfulness. No matter where you are, speeding past roadside attractions, counting milestones, or approaching an intersection of life, resilience and mental toughness reside within you, awaiting the call to duty. The key to developing as a resilient individual is to step back, pause, breathe, and reflect on your own unique path and true north. Enjoy the journey.

MASTER YOUR MINDSET: Your Destiny

✦ What skills do you need to develop in order to elevate from leader to coach?

✦ In what way do you need to flip your own script?

✦ How do you define and find "balance" in your life?

PART 2

THE FUNDAMENTALS

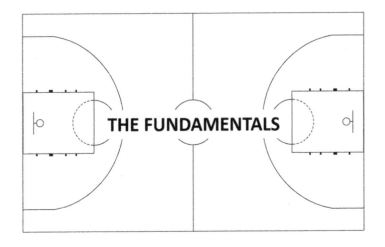

5

Getting Serious

"Happiness is no laughing matter."
–RICHARD WHATELY–

During my NCAA coaching career, I lived at the speed of light and consumed myself in the daily rat race of collegiate athletics, drinking from a fire hose. I either felt satisfied and happy, or frustrated and disappointed. Much of my mental status depended on the daily fire alarms, the wins and losses, and the near-term impact I was having on the people around me. At the time, I did not have the ability to understand, vocabulary to describe it, or the perspective to manage what actually was happening when it related to my overall emotional health, my well-being, and my happiness.

Rearview Mirror

Today I can look back, put all of the pieces together, and sort out what my happiness looked like, felt like, and the contributing factors. Looking back then and looking ahead now, I understand that happiness is a serious business. It is a foundational element to our mental health. As we strengthen and sustain happiness, intentional practice and training in the form of "exercise" make a difference in our emotional health and well-being.

Happiness does not get the respect it deserves; in fact, most of us take it for granted and typically experience it passively, like a warm summer breeze passing through. It is rarely seen as a powerful business trait for increasing results. It is the goal that initiates our drive, energy, and motivation to be the best. It should be taken seriously and we need to take our own personal happiness inventory often. This must be part of our overall fitness plan and one to which we commit. Do not leave happiness to chance and think you can just wait for it like the passing breeze.

Many people expect someone else to "give" them happiness. We do not take personal responsibility and many think happiness will be delivered like a Christmas present. Some play a victim's role and feel others are just luckier than they are. We blame others for dissatisfaction, lack of happiness, and limited success, and we refuse to take responsibility and ownership. What we learn and find out throughout life is that we create our own luck and happiness. No one can take happiness away from you; you can only give it away.

I spent a considerable amount of time examining my own thoughts and feelings from almost three decades of coaching. This gave me a new perspective and context about the "secret of my success" and enabled me to apply it moving forward. Typical big-time coaches all come from the same mold; Type A, driven, tenacious, and ambitious, we want to be the best, we are ultra-competitive, and we hate to lose. We have a certain DNA type and are wired differently than most.

> *No one can take happiness away from you.*
> *You can only give it away.*

Spending time alone in thought has been a positive and rich opportunity for my personal growth and creativity. Others may commit time but their thoughts turn negative, turning against themselves critically which becomes unproductive and dangerous. Introspection is a process of healthy self-reflection, examination, meditation, and exploration. It comes with many benefits for our overall well-being. It is a way to understand ourselves by turning inward and appreciating our own true selves.

My client Marcia was a high performer within an organization of 40,000 employees. In her early thirties, Marcia managed a product line regulated by the Food and Drug Administration. She was the only individual in this organization who was qualified, certified, and credentialed for this position. She was early in her career and managed a large team. The demands were high and the expectations of flawless quality control were at an all-time high. Her integrity in following rules, policies, and federal guidelines and regulations were on point. However, Marcia experienced misalignment in managing the pressure from her supervisor for how quickly products got out the door.

During the onboarding process of our coaching engagement, I learned that Marcia's emotional health and well-being were very low, particularly in her emotional capacity and mental strength. After I presented her the report, following several interviews, conversations, and assessments, we set goals and areas of growth over the next nine months to increase overall emotional intelligence and take action around increasing her well-being and happiness. She set specific goals and committed her effort and we built in multiple benchmarks to celebrate the wins and to increase self-awareness for any missed opportunities for growth. As Marcia pivoted to take responsibility for her own well-being, she felt an increasing and transformative level of happiness and positive attitude.

Her experience and growth proved what is possible by shifting our mindset and committing and implementing strategies daily to positively affect our own happiness. We conducted a "before" and "after" assessment as metrics and return on investment using the same EQ assessment tool. Her scores improved by 27 points in nine months! Marcia started in the low range and skyrocketed to the high range to put herself in a position as an exceptional performer and leader in the workplace and to enhance her overall well-being. She fully bought in to the process and did the work to get the results she wanted and needed. She not only came extremely prepared to our meetings, she did the work on her own outside of our coaching sessions. What makes a difference and really matters, for corporate and elite athletes, is the work and practice that gets done when the coach is not watching.

Developing a high competency of resilience serves as an indicator and measurement of overall happiness, satisfaction, and well-being. Our happiness can be used as a barometer of our own emotional and mental health in the journey to discover the best version of ourselves. Building a reserve of limitless resilience is important so we can access it any time. This is not only how we survive, but how we thrive consistently no matter what adversity or setbacks we face.

Health and Wellness in Sports and Life

Professional and Olympic athletes leverage training and development of emotional and mental health and wellness widely. When working with and developing athletes, these elite athletes' coaches may ask themselves an important question: *How self-aware are they and what level is their emotional intelligence skills and competencies?* Coaches are expected to be role models, set an example, make a positive impact, and bring out the best in their athletes and teams. However, many coaches are unfamiliar with mental and emotional wellness competencies and have not developed the necessary life-long skills that could be the difference of one being retained or fired. Coaching styles and approaches historically have trended toward control, power, and manipulative approaches.

In today's environment, a successful coach must master the skills to balance the blurry line between winning at a very high level consistently and managing the daily challenges of a new generation with different expectations. This skillset reaches beyond the X's and O's on which most coaches focus; however, learning and developing the ability to facilitate emotional and mental intelligence will make them better coaches—and enable their athletes to perform better. The mistake is thinking this activity is linear, like incrementally learning and practicing a physical skill. Being able to manage people, lead a program, and enable an entire staff and players to perform at the highest level every day is not about X's and O's.

Most athletes perceive their coaches completely differently than coaches perceive themselves. A coach's level of competency strongly influences the level of an athlete's well-being, happiness, and emotional wellness. More than ever before, these skills and abilities play a huge role in athletic performance and contribute significantly to a coach's success. We are all driven, but not in the same way. Understanding and leveraging the motives behind why and what we do represent important elements to holistically impact individual and team success. Instead of overemphasizing physical or technical skills, we should invest resources and focus our time on developing emotional and mental performance capabilities. When you do, positive outcomes and expected results for yourself and the organization will follow.

Every athletic coach tells you they will win and that they will accomplish special things; it is just the way coaches communicate and carry themselves. Parents can tell right away if a coach can help their child develop on and off the court, holistically. For a collegiate coach, the ability to sign top rated recruits is critical, but real success entails the ability to develop overall physical, mental, and emotional skills that translate to life success. *What do the best coaches say? What makes their communication and ability to find that fine line so different from all the others?* Coaches who develop the whole athlete—physical, mental, and emotional—differentiate themselves and produce higher-level results.

Some coaches may guarantee playing time, dangling the carrot of immediacy in the faces of recruits. This gets the attention of young athletes hungering for stardom and attention. However, most parents and athletes do not realize the best offer is an opportunity to compete and to develop and grow skills not just during the four years in college, but to enable the athlete to excel for forty (or more) years. As a coach I would say, *You're going to get a chance to come and compete for a spot, and to train with and play with and against the best.* By issuing a challenge instead of promising a handout, my approach attracted those who wanted to be challenged and coached at the highest level. That appealed to my competitive nature and, in the long run, their overall happiness and well-being.

> *Coaches who develop the whole athlete—physical,
> mental, and emotional—differentiate themselves
> and produce higher-level results.*

For all my players and coaches, the message was clear: everything is earned. I believed in the process. I did not differ much from a sales leader fully bought into my product. I had faith in our system to win at a high level, so the culture we created and the conviction I had poured out into the living rooms of recruits and their families. The passion and motive in my message and tone was of love, passion, authenticity, and happiness that would extend to their overall growth and development and would serve as a springboard for the rest of their lives.

The Secret to My Success

Reflecting on the past, I discovered the secret to my success by looking internally. The more I learned about myself, the more I recognized the fine line between competitiveness and gratitude within me. My drive, passion, and ambition were ingrained as I strived to be the best. At the same time, I felt grateful, appreciative, and thankful for the path I took. Can you relate to and understand where I am coming from? Elite, high performers are never satisfied; they are careful not to get complacent and others who surround and push them to the next level. We must balance the thinking that things are never good enough with the knowledge that perfection is unattainable because we want to be and be around the best. This fine line drives me to continue to learn and to grow and serves as motivation for many of us.

I realized at some point during my journey that I had to find a balance. I was on the razor's edge with my drive to be the best, while working hard to appreciate where I was and what I had accomplished. One of the pillars of happiness is embracing learning and growth that aligns with your values. Self-motivation and feelings of an enriched life ultimately drive our satisfaction and overall happiness. If we appreciate only the winning results at the end of a season, we will be disappointed for much of our personal and professional life.

Lean into the process and value all the experiences and milestones on the journey. If we can be fulfilled and happy in the moment and embrace the process, we will enjoy the journey a lot more. The key is finding your passion, then the drive and the work ethic to be the best follow. We all need to take ownership and responsibility for our happiness, health, and well-being.

One thing we can change today is how we take control and accept responsibility moving forward. We are all unique and define what happiness and success look like in our lives. *What are we willing to change and do differently moving forward?* There are many factors that determine our happiness and well-being. We all have experienced hardships and setbacks, some more than others. We may reflect on past experiences that were positive to help us get through tough times and to remind ourselves that each of us are a work in progress. We must discover our own true north. If we do not, no one else will.

In a team or an organization, culture creates (or negates) a holistic approach to reach peak performance. At the individual and team level, embracing a more agile approach in our own lives when we need to shift and to reprioritize our goals is part of the process. There are many times I needed to pivot during different stages of my life in order to reach my goals personally and professionally. And when I did, I was more successful in creating an environment for others around me to thrive.

We can learn and further develop the skills and abilities tied to our overall happiness. We can improve and strengthen them by focusing on doing the work. We tend to be reactive instead of proactive; we must not wait until we hit rock bottom to invest in ourselves. By that time, the deep hole we have dug makes the climb out even harder. In my consulting work, I have observed that many of the issues confronting individuals and organizations could be prevented through proactive planning, a strategy set in motion, and continuous learning and adjustment. Instead, lack of attention to well-being can produce devastating results. Faulty communication, an unhealthy culture, disengagement, poor leadership, complacency, and lack of human skills are just a few of the most common problems. These issues and challenges create unnecessary stress, anxiety, fear and uncertainty on a daily basis. Be proactive and address these issues.

Why do some people seem to possess a greater capacity for emotional strength? Why are some people able to achieve success and happiness in life better than others? Why do some people blessed with high intellectual abilities seem to fail quickly, while others who have modest intellectual gifts succeed? Unsuccessful senior-level leaders fail because they put strategy before people. Successful leaders rise and elevate when they have a high competency of emotional intelligence. They show people acumen, build trust easily, communicate effectively, put an importance on building relationships, and solve problems quickly.

Take some time to think about what makes you happy. Little things may create enjoyment like a great cup of coffee, a bowl of a favorite ice cream, listening to a playlist, shopping at a favorite store, working out, being outdoors, or reading a favorite author's new book. On a broader scale you may find deeper satisfaction from activities such as vacationing with friends and family, volunteering in the community, or mentoring others. Our "happy list" may be small and specific—or it can be enormous and expansive—but we all should have a go-to list.

Much of my senior executive coaching is based on research, positive psychology, training, and real experience working with elite athletes and clients who have experienced life-changing results. Defining our own happiness represents the best way forward. *But how do we define something that seems so intangible, like happiness?* Research and experience provide us with four fundamentals to increase our level of happiness, well-being, and emotional health. A high competency in each help limit or may prevent derailments we could face. If we work intentionally on strengthening these fundamental elements and they become daily habits, our overall well-being can become limitless.

Fundamental #1: Self-Regard

Do we forgive ourselves when we make mistakes? Do we appreciate ourselves when we learn a skill or perform effectively? While it may seem strange and even "self-centered" to focus attention on ourselves, self-regard is critical for life success. From middle school to the boardroom, it is a life-long journey to develop an ability to recognize our strengths and limitations and to feel good about ourselves. People who respect and accept themselves, like the way they are, and are comfortable in their own skin are being true to themselves.

Does this sound like a skill you would like to develop and master? Individuals with high self-regard own their strengths and limitations; they feel inner strength, independence, self-assuredness, self-confidence, secure, and self-reliant. These individuals have developed an appreciation for and acknowledgment of accurately gauging their strengths and also opportunities for growth. As we embrace and realize all of our strengths, we can leverage and capitalize on them in the moment and over the long term.

> *Individuals with high self-regard own their strengths and limitations; they feel inner strength, independence, self-assuredness, self-confidence, secure, and self-reliant.*

Realizing our strengths helps us increase our level of self-confidence. Individuals with high self-regard also have no trouble owning their mistakes and failures, taking responsibility. With an awareness of and commitment to improve on our limitations, we find an even greater sense of self-sufficiency as we tackle our crooked rims head on. Feeling sure of oneself depends on self-respect, self-esteem, and a well-developed sense of self.

People who are fulfilled have a positive outlook on life, are satisfied with who they are, and have strong self-regard. Individuals who feel inadequate experience a crisis of confidence, are insecure, and need to focus on and to develop self-regard in their lives. Nadia Levus and Ivan Franko captured the benefit of positive self-regard in their research article (*Journal of Education, Culture and Society*, December 2012), stating "Positive self-regard is accompanied by growth of creativity level. Creativity becomes a certain skill that helps overcome stressful situations . . . Among the creative skills and abilities foregrounded are creative approach, curiosity and creative intuition." Self-regard is a game changer and sets a foundation to do what we love and to enjoy success and happiness.

Self-regard is critical to overall well-being and happiness. Take the time to explore and identify your strengths, what you like about yourself, and strategies you can work on immediately. Throughout our lives we will experience situations, positions, and roles where we must lean on the self-regard competency to boost our confidence and to take us to the next level. The higher we climb the ladder, the more well-developed and unflappable this powerful skill must be. Very successful people and teams know how they excel and the gaps and blind spots that may limit them. As coaches, we build high-performing teams and surround ourselves with others who are even better and stronger—people who fill our gaps and complement our strengths.

If you want to feel more satisfied with your life and accomplishments, increase your self-regard as one of your personal and professional development goals. It will require a high degree of self-awareness and an investment of time to examine what you do well and to understand your limitations. The better you know yourself and leverage your strengths, the more confident you will be in your immediate and long-term interactions. From the athletes I coached to middle managers and C-suite executives I guide today, achieving self-regard has made a long-term impact in their lives. It is the cornerstone fundamental.

Fundamental #2: Optimism

Do you see the bright side of things or get mired in the muck? In the middle of adversity or crisis, do you succumb to the fear or revel in the challenge? Optimism is more than just an emotional state of mind; it is a skill that should be a mandatory competency and necessary aspect of our lives. Optimism, like hope, entails having a strong sense and an expectation in what is possible, knowing that situations will turn out all right despite adversity, doubt, setbacks, and failures. As we develop the key skills that determine our personal and professional success, optimism is a mindset that shields us against hopelessness and depression while it lifts us to higher performance in any circumstance.

A high level of optimism serves as a tool and go-to attribute to help us manage the smallest setback or the greatest failure. Those of us with a high level of optimism see failure as growth—an opportunity that will only make us better. Those without optimism view failures as roadblocks and express an impossibility to change the circumstances they experience. Our reaction represents the hallmark of our level of optimism, such as how we respond to losing a game, getting fired, being turned down for a job, or blowing a presentation. Optimistic people accept the challenge and seek out help, a coach, or advice and use the setback as an opportunity to grow and get better. People who lack optimism bemoan the circumstances, retreat from the challenge, and waste energy on fear and complaint.

Having the tools to cope in stressful situations, seeing stress as an opportunity to make us better, and manifesting a positive attitude are game changers. We all have experienced different levels of stress throughout our lives and it impacts us all in different ways. We must have the ability to manage and to embrace stress, to flourish in a crisis, and to perform when expectations are high. If we cannot, we find ourselves in a position of high risk and get derailed as individuals and leaders.

> *Optimistic people accept the challenge and seek out help, a coach, or advice and use the setback as an opportunity to grow and get better. People who lack optimism bemoan the circumstances, retreat from the challenge, and waste energy on fear and complaint.*

Consider the value of optimism to a salesperson. When optimism is a strength for a salesperson, that individual typically has an emotional intelligence mindset with the ability to listen to and to empathize with their customers' needs. Along the client development cycle, sales professionals pile up the "No" responses and they must have a reserve of optimistic motivation and positive attitude to continue. In sports, slumping shooters need to have the attitude that they must continue to shoot. In baseball, a great player makes an out about 70 percent of the time. Football kickers who have missed a few field goals in a row and who are iced with just seconds remaining on the clock must step up and have the attitude and ability to regroup and nail the kick. If our optimism is low, a positive outlook is unlikely. *How can we reframe situations in a more positive light? Are you aware that your less-than-positive outlook has an effect on others?*

People who have a sense of self-efficacy bounce back from failure quickly. They move on to the next play in seconds and have a "short memory" for mistakes. A common attribute of their successful approach is to focus on how they will address situations rather than to worry about all the things that could go wrong. Optimistic people are resilient and hardy; they face adversity with a realistic "can do" attitude and mindset. Rather than giving up and running away from difficulties, they persevere and know that with grit, anything is possible.

Carolyn Youssef and Fred Luthans conducted and published a study paper addressing "Positive Organizational Behavior in the Workplace: The Impact of Hope, Optimism, and Resilience" (*Journal of Management*, 2007). The research study of more than 1,032 employees at all positional levels from 135 Midwestern companies, across multiple industries and sectors, focused on training and development interventions related to positivity and resilience. Using experimental designs, broad cross-sectional samples, and training programs for specific companies, even finite, short-term interventions (e.g., a training workshop) significantly increased the level of the participants' psychological capacities by 1.5 percent to 3.0 percent, whereas control groups not receiving the training opportunity showed no increase. Data in an analysis with engineering managers in a large high-tech manufacturing firm showed a 270% return on investment from this positivity intervention. If a short-term positivity training session produces such results, imagine if you and your organization build positive psychology into ongoing team leadership, skills development, and individual and team management. The results could be limitless.

Developing into a driven and caring individual and leader takes shifting our mindset toward optimism and implementing an intentional practice plan to enhance it. There is power in positive thinking and optimism can be learned and developed as part of our daily mental exercise routine. While it may seem hard to shift your mentality in the face of adversity, optimism represents one of the most beneficial skills to impact your physical and emotional wellness—and it can make a big impact on all those around you.

Fundamental #3: Relationships

Who makes a difference in your life? Who can you count on and share success and challenges? Developing mutually satisfying relationships, especially in the workplace, can be rewarding and enjoyable, and benefit employee engagement and results. Strong relationships enable both give and take, and behavior and actions demonstrate trust, respect, understanding, and compassion. For well-being and mental health, we benefit from fulfilling relationships that offer us the support and encouragement we need through the good times and the bad. This is also true at home in our relationships with our spouse and outside the home with friends and in our roles in church or the community. For true fulfillment, mutually satisfying relationships at home and work are important to bring harmony and a connectedness to our lives.

We have all been in relationships where it has been all "give" and we feel like we do not get the same "give" back. We have also been in relationships where it has been all "take" or we are the ones who are the takers. To feel a connectedness and satisfaction in our lives, we must have mutually beneficial relationships with others. Having the focus and understanding the importance of a mutually beneficial relationship is the first step. Building relationships is more important than technical skills in driving our own and others' success.

Having the ability and skillset to connect and to build relationships with others is a necessity and is expected in every position in every industry. It should be on every job description and serve as a key aspect of our health report card. Some of us interact with others and connect exceptionally well in the workplace and in social settings. There are also many people who experience discomfort socially and struggle to develop those connections easily. Connectedness takes work, so find a method that works for you and get comfortable being uncomfortable in order to achieve a higher level of happiness and well-being.

> *People who are significant in our lives play an integral role in supporting, mentoring, and helping us reach our goals that we may have never been able to achieve on our own. And when we connect with and help others, we experience an even higher degree of fulfillment.*

With evolving technology and work structures, many people today are working remotely—or are in cubicles or offices all day—without connecting and socializing with others. The absence of fulfilling relationships represents a hazard for remote workers and others who find themselves in permanent virtual work situations.

Extra effort is required to cultivate and to develop deep and meaningful relationships in today's workplace. We have our family at home and we need to have our work family also to experience richness in our lives.

Kristin Ryba summarizes relationship-building benefits for business in her Quantum Workplace article, "Building Relationships at Work: Why It Matters" (June 2019). She summarizes four key findings from a review of research and data:

1. Employees are more satisfied. Employee satisfaction increases nearly 50% when a worker develops a close relationship on the job.
2. Managers are less stressed. Managers experience significantly less stress when they feel they have a good relationship with their employees.
3. Employees manage conflicts better. Studies show that conflict leads to lost time and less effort at work, while relationships enable more rapid and effective conflict resolution.
4. Employee desires are met. Relationships with coworkers are among the top drivers of employee engagement—77% of employees list them as a priority.

Developing mutually satisfying relationships has many business benefits and it is a differentiator for our mental and emotional health; the professional gains in our status, job advancement, and performance results should not be overlooked as a relationship benefit. People who are significant in our lives play an integral role in supporting, mentoring, and helping us reach our goals that we may have never been able to achieve on our own. And when we connect with and help others, we experience an even higher degree of fulfillment.

Fundamental #4: Self-Actualization

What are you most passionate about? Where are you headed in your work and life and what actions are you taking to get there? Setting goals and continually improving yourself leads to a happier and richer life. Pursuing meaningful goals is a lifelong journey as we strive to live life to its fullest. This need does not change as we continue to advance and to experience different chapters in our life; in fact, it is often the difference between being stuck and making progress.

We must beware of becoming complacent, especially later in life, or we may lose. We may lose the feeling of satisfaction, happiness, and the ability to realize our potential and capabilities. We may lose tangibly, such as our marriage or our financial status or our physical health. Striving to reach our potential while developing purpose and meaning is a life-long journey. Driving forward to our maximum development in our abilities, talents, and strengths provides excitement and produces a feeling of self-satisfaction. This is integral for our own individual well-being; we earn self-respect and pride through a willingness to learn and grow and to strive to reach our peak potential.

> *Being a life-long learner, staying curious, and feeling like you have never arrived sustain motivation and excitement about growth potential.*

Our values change at different stages of our lives. Our self-motivation ultimately drives life achievement and our overall happiness. *What does self-actualization have to do with your success in life?* Quite a lot, actually. The most successful people are aware of the goals, behaviors, actions, and relationships that give them energy and excite them. Are you using your talents, skills, and gifts at your optimal level? If we get too comfortable, living too contented of a life, we may feel a void that will not only impact our own life, but it may impact those around you.

It is no surprise that elite athletes develop a strong competency in self-actualization. The best and most successful athletes focus on maximizing their talents and reaching their optimal level of performance. They are passionate about getting better, about reaching their potential and becoming the best at what they do. Their long-term goals are a destination, and they focus on the journey. Being a life-long learner, staying curious, and feeling like you have never arrived sustain motivation and excitement about growth potential. When we continue to strive for more, we find new horizons in work and in other aspects of our personal life.

As human beings, we have basic psychological needs for personal growth and development throughout our lives. By focusing on self-actualization, we can find meaning and purpose in our lives and are able to say we truly lived. Take responsibility for your path in life and travel toward new horizons constantly.

* * *

Stacking these four fundamentals creates a foundation to strengthen our resilience and offers a path forward to taking responsibility for our happiness. *But what happens when our own behaviors or shortcomings conspire to derail us? Can we stay the course or do we get off-track?* Remaining committed to strengthening our foundation steels us to battle against our own derailers and ensures that we emphasize the beliefs and behaviors that increase our satisfaction and happiness.

A derailer is a weakness and if not addressed or minimized, more than likely, it will prevent us from achieving success and our true potential. Derailers are part of our journey; expect them to surface and have the courage to engage in your own growth and development. Most derailers are more than just minor weaknesses and they require immediate attention especially in stress, during crises, and under pressure. They become a "fatal flaw" when not corrected immediately.

Do not let derailer behaviors stand in the way of your progress. We all have weaknesses that we may never choose to improve or attempt to master. Decades of research suggests that it is very difficult to change core aspects of your personality after the age of 30. But you can tame the dark side of derailers in critical situations by changing your behaviors, focusing on these four fundamentals, self-regard, optimism, relationships, and self-actualization. Control what you can control—yourself and your growth—and make it a priority in your busy life.

MASTER YOUR MINDSET: Your Well-Being

+ How do you take time to improve your mental and emotional well-being?

+ How will you take responsibility for your own happiness?

+ What single action are you committed to take in each of the four fundamentals today?

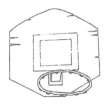

6

Thriving Through Adversity

"I've grown most not from victories, but setbacks."
—Serena Williams—

Developing a positive mindset to embrace setbacks and thriving in spite of them are critical to overcome adversity. My experience in college athletics demonstrated the power of positivity. As a basketball coach and later in business, I decided to help others rise, to pull others up instead as the world and others tried to push them down and tear them apart. Who will help us rise unless we rise together as a team? We do not accomplish anything special or significant on our own without the support of others—a tribe, a village, a team.

Rising Together

I was coaching at the University of Minnesota when I founded TeamWomen (TW) in 2011. TW, a Twin Cities nonprofit organization, has become the resource for every woman and girl to learn, grow, connect, and become their best selves. We all have experienced success, and some setbacks, throughout our lives. Through TW, we wanted to build an organization that provides a team atmosphere and environment to strengthen confidence, to broaden networks, and to provide mentoring and development opportunities across industries. My motivation to start TW came from other successful women who arrived at the top of their industries after surviving many setbacks throughout their lives, personally and professionally. Their ability to battle through setbacks paved their often-bumpy road to success, and some of TW's early participants earned Top 50 leadership awards in the Twin Cities.

Setbacks often provide an opportunity to learn and to grow. In early 2020, the world was hit with a 100-year pandemic. The TW organization, as leaders in the community, decided to provide resources and opportunities to connect and to support each other during this crisis. So many were struggling to figure out how to survive and many faced a multitude of setbacks in their lives. As the organization pulled together, everyone shared their own life-changing stories of devastation, fear, and loss ranging from financial pain to critical health challenges including death—and everything in between. Many people gathered several days each month, virtually, and in creative ways with social distancing. They were determined to embrace fear and the unknown by building strength and rising together, mining for hope and opportunity in a deep pit of darkness.

Resilience is having the tools and skills to bounce back after mistakes, failures, and adversity. In sports, games are full of mistakes and turnovers, recruits who say no, players who transfer, bad calls by the officials, and surprising upsets. It is an expectation to learn how to "move on to the next play" quickly, often within seconds. As a coach, you must develop a high-level of resilience and mental toughness to fail with grace and to demonstrate stability and strength. When the cameras are rolling, the spotlight is bright, and all eyes are on you, the leader as coach has a responsibility to teach and to instill these traits in their players. To build a resilient team, the coach must lead the fight and battle through adversity to win with grace.

> *The best players were expected to practice harder and we put them into situations to experience more adversity from their coaches and teammates—as leaders we needed more from them.*

Dynamic change, routine adversity, and periodic chaos are the norm in sports. The best coaches create an environment for players to experience worst-case scenarios, stress, and pressure situations in practice. In my coaching career, we planned our practices to create scenarios more difficult than what players would experience in a game. People do not believe me when I tell them that practices were always longer and harder than games. The best players also were expected to practice harder and we put them into situations to experience more adversity from their coaches and teammates—as leaders we needed more from them. During practice, players are formed and strengthened, and they developed confidence, prepared for adversity, and stretched their comfort zones.

On game day, players and coaches react and perform based on the training that conditions their bodies, minds, and instincts. Again, mastering their mindset happens in practice and during training—high-performing athletes do not just show up in the bright lights of show time without proper preparation and readiness for adversity. They are prepared and they believe every time they step on the floor that they are the best. They do not look at setbacks as failure, because no matter how great you are, there will always be setbacks. As you prepare for show time, and get into the game, expect adversity and setbacks and make sure you build a nice cushion of confidence to fall back on.

Fearless Hope

Resilience is not a skill that is "one and done". We live in unprecedented times. It requires constant and consistent learning, training, and development to navigate the complex and ever-changing world in which we live. Making it through challenges teaches us to be comfortable being uncomfortable and strengthens one of the most important relationships we have—the one we have with ourselves. Still, there are moments in life for which no training or development can prepare us and in which resilience is the only answer.

That moment for me came late one night and close to bedtime when the phone rang. It was my Dad and he delivered the news that my little sister, Lisa, had cancer. After I hung up, I dropped to my knees in the middle of the kitchen, put my head in my hands, and wept. And I was terrified. Fear paralyzes us but it also can catapult us into a place of greater faith. That greater faith demands bravery when adversity stares us in the face. Throughout her ordeal, Lisa was fearless and the most courageous person I have ever met to this day. Her inner wisdom and faith buoyed her spirits—and ours—and kept her in the fight.

Initially, I was in disbelief and could not believe it was happening—not to my little sister. Lisa was diagnosed with Stage 4 colon cancer in the fall of 2017 after she turned 50 years old. We have a family history of colon cancer and my sister drew the short straw out of the four kids. I felt guilty and wondered, *Why not me?* I wanted to take away her pain and make it my own. Big sisters are supposed to protect their younger sisters. How did this happen? As an older sister, the joys and pains of having a little sister are experienced universally. No one ever picked on Lisa . . . except for me. I was that older sister shaking my head at my younger siblings, or they were rolling their eyes at me.

When Lisa learned about her cancer, she sold her home and moved back to the Ohio farm to live with my parents. My business was firing on all cylinders and I was traveling three weeks out of the month, meeting with clients and speaking. Fortunately, my second career in business gave me flexibility to slow down and to engage with my family. Instead of returning home at the end of my trips, I shifted my home base to the Ohio farm for four months.

This puts a strain on most relationships, but my spouse had just lost her oldest brother to cancer a year before. I am forever grateful to Lynn for understanding my need to abandon our lives and for allowing me to spend time with Lisa and my family. I remember stopping at my house in Pennsylvania only a couple of times for a few hours to check in, to get some clean clothes, and to get centered. I would drive six hours to my parents' farm every break I had to be by my sister's side and to help my parents.

Throughout my entire life I learned more from my parents than anyone else. They taught me many traits that I highlighted in my first book, *On Point*, and during Lisa's battle I observed my parents modeling their strength and resilience physically, mentally, emotionally, and spiritually every day. I will never forget and always cherish that time and it will forever be etched in my mind. If I were still coaching college basketball, I would have not had the amount of time to spend her final months with her. After three decades of being absent in much of her life, time was a gift I had been given with her.

My parents taught me life lessons once again, now as an adult. I watched them with love, compassion, and appreciation as they put their lives on hold for two years to support my sister through her adversity. Lisa spent her final four months in hospice care at home and my parents were her caretakers. I witnessed a side of them I had never seen before as they both prepared in their own ways for their child's eventual death.

In the face of setbacks, deep sadness, and disappointments, the ability to regroup and reclaim a happy state relies on one's level of optimism. Optimism is one of my gifts and a strength I have developed and mastered throughout my life. When a person demonstrates a high level of optimism, and adopts a positive mental framework during setbacks, the approach and their outlook on life enhances and sustains happiness. For our overall well-being and as a tool to weather setbacks, optimism represents one of the most critical and effective capabilities—and it is 100 percent learnable through practice and training.

I believe things happen for a reason and that we all have a purpose. Lisa was always purpose driven and she experienced clarity through her faith. During the precious time I spent with my sister during her illness, she taught me so much about hope, bravery, and resilience. I memorized her movements, I listened to her words, and I observed her actions; she was suffering but would always claim she was not in pain. This front-row seat offered me more lessons than any other learning I had—not from the crooked rim, not between the four lines in The Barn, and not during my certification classes from world-renowned teachers who were the gurus globally on resilience, hope, and grit. On top of Lisa's journey, I watched my parents—78 and 80 years old—handle constant heart ache, show empathy and compassion, and physically take care of her. It was a classroom I would never choose voluntarily . . . and I could never place a value on what I learned.

My sister fearlessly approached her journey with undeniable strength, smiling through all the pain and disappointments. Despite the advanced-stage cancer, she never gave up and always had hope. She believed there would be a way for her to beat cancer with chemotherapy, clinical trials, surgery, a miracle, and prayer. Lisa's hope showed me for the first time in my life that hope could take hold and bolster the desire to live. She believed from the beginning in miracles and, through an unwavering commitment to hope, her situation became more bearable and stay motivated and fought.

I always thought I was the toughest one in the family—but I was wrong. And did I mention that Lisa was still going to work at least three to four days a week for eight hours a day during her illness? *How many people do you know with Stage 4 colon cancer who would work until their last four months of life?* For months, my Dad dropped her off and picked her up from work, made her scrambled eggs every morning for breakfast, and drove her from hospital to hospital, treatment to treatment, from one specialist to the next. She was turned down from several clinical trials, she switched doctors, we got second opinions, she attempted surgery, all while working full time. My sister held onto hope and put her trust in her faith and in her purpose. It was excruciating—and illuminating and inspiring.

We Will Never Forget

As I observed my sister's strength, witnessed her grit, and monitored the decisions she made until her final months, I asked myself, *Would I have been able to endure that?* At the same time, I have never witnessed more mental and emotional strength than from my parents. Setback after setback tested Lisa and my parents every day and they persevered and fought to the bitter end.

Lisa spent the last 15 months of her life at the farm and, fittingly, it is where she took her last breath. Her final trip home from the hospital was immediately to hospice care on the farm. I will never forget Lisa's final words a couple hours before she passed away. She turned toward me and said, *Pam, I love you and I am so proud of you.* My last words to my little sister were, *I love you too, I have always been proud of you and I will never ever forget you.*

I will never forget those four months on the farm: reeling from deep sadness, crying together, and having tough conversations. Lisa helped plan her own funeral, my parents fed and bathed her, and we made sure she had everything she needed. She died peacefully right next to my parents. Preparing for and watching their child die is something a parent should never have to endure.

Before Lisa died, we promised we would construct a memorial in her honor at the church. We installed a large digital sign on the church's front lawn where she attended services every Sunday morning. Today, this beautiful sign lights up the sky and projects messages that serve and bring the entire community together.

Thank you, Lisa and Mom and Dad. We will never forget.

Slipping Into Danger

It was her senior year, and one of my players slid into a cycle of decline without even knowing it. Eventually, a pattern of poor performance and physical and emotional behavior became visible to everyone. The symptoms and behavior got harder to manage and to ignore and her issues started to affect her overall health and well-being. I knew something was seriously wrong off the court, and it was affecting her overall performance academically and athletically. Time was running out and so were her stories and excuses.

We learned through some of her teammates that she was in an abusive relationship with her boyfriend. Teammates know everything about each other and they were protecting her by keeping it quiet. She just finished an All-Big Ten junior year as one of the top players in the conference and was primed to have an even stronger senior year. Every time we asked her—if she was ok, if she needed help, if we could do anything for her, if she would say what was going on—she would claim that everything was fine. She would make excuses about school, homework, and time management, and she began doing extra workouts and getting in the gym more to hone her skills.

As the weeks went by, she started losing weight, she became irritable, and she requested medication from our sports medicine team to help her focus longer and better. Where there's smoke there's fire, and we were seeing billowing smoke. The straw that broke the camel's back was the day she walked into practice with a bruise on her face and her left hand wrapped in athletic tape. I gasped and knew it was time to sound the alarm. Her boyfriend had hit her the night before during an argument and she reacted by punching the wall.

Finally, a deliberate choice needed to be made. She had spiraled out of control to the point where I was unsure if could get her turned around for the season. Symptoms of depression were starting to surface including weight loss, fatigue, low self-esteem, insomnia, and an inability to concentrate. Between the stress and pressure she had put on herself to have a great season, the traumatic events she experienced off the court, and the anxiety she felt every day, we could see her slipping into a dangerous place. Basketball took a backseat and many people intervened so she could function as a healthy young adult and student first.

Fortunately, tools and strategies often can help people manage anxiety, depression, and post-traumatic stress disorder (PTSD) symptoms and conditions without medication. Medication may offer a short-term remedy when supported by drug-free treatments backed by science. As she addressed the conditions and began improving, there were intense conversations about developing purpose and meaning in her life and about controlling negative thought patterns. The goal was to help her strengthen her self-regard, to enhance her optimism, and to surround herself with the right people. Her relationships were not healthy and were causing physical and mental health issues. Healthy and mutually satisfying relationships are critical to our overall well-being and happiness.

> *Tools and strategies often can help people manage anxiety, depression, and post-traumatic stress disorder (PTSD) symptoms and conditions without medication.*

She worked closely with our support staff to remove herself from her damaging off-court environment and she eagerly started implementing strategies daily to retrain her mindset. She was getting enough exercise each day, which is an important lifestyle change to build and to sustain good mental health. In addition, she committed to daily mindfulness practice to strengthen her mindset and to retrain her thought patterns to remain present in the moment with full focus, without reacting emotionally. She made continual progress and recovered her strength, her self-esteem, and her ability to engage in school and on the court.

* * *

Fortunately, major failures and severe issues come along infrequently in life. Retraining our mind allows us to bounce back quickly from the frequent minor mistakes, setbacks, and adversity that are routine in our lives. Setbacks will always weave through life, but they do not have to define who we are. We have a choice on what legacy we want to leave behind. Setbacks come and go and some last longer than others and are more intense. No matter the setback—major or minor—how we respond and react helps shape who we are and what we may become.

Life can be difficult and even heart-breaking. It was for me. But with time and practice, I learned that addressing life's pitfalls is a continuous process and a journey that serves to deepen and to strengthen my resilience. I committed to take care of myself first, so I could be at my best for others. You can develop the knowledge, skills, and the confidence to handle whatever comes your way. The choice is up to you, so when you have decided, get to work.

MASTER YOUR MINDSET: Your Challenges

+ What major personal and professional challenges have you faced and what lessons did you learn?

+ How can you increase your optimism and belief in what is possible?

+ What setbacks have you mishandled or allowed to take you off-track? What would you do differently if you had a "do-over"?

7

Mastering the Pivot Move

*"Opportunities to find deeper powers within ourselves
come when life seems most challenging."*
–JOSEPH CAMPBELL–

TIME OUT! Time out! My players hustled over to the bench. I walked into the huddle and prepared to draw up a play on the dry erase clipboard. I gave the players a minute to towel off, get water, and talk with each other before I spoke. Over the years, I'd learned the importance of allowing players to have a minute to communicate about what is happening out on the court before they hear from me. In this moment, yet another turnover was showing up as frustration in the huddle. My time out was designed to help us pivot.

Pivoting to Success

We were struggling to take care of the ball, with a dozen turn-overs already. Half of our turnovers resulted from traveling violations—maybe a sign of nerves or perhaps the players were just moving too quickly without purpose. My captain leaned over to one of my star freshman guards and demanded, *TAKE CARE OF THE BALL. Brittany, when you are being pressured, do not pick up your dribble! If you are getting trapped, pivot away from the defense to get a better passing angle . . . WE ARE OPEN! COME ON!*

My captain was holding everyone accountable for their roles and responsibilities in the game. The players argued back and forth, competitive energy flowing freely. Finally, I stepped in for the remainder of the timeout. In a calm tone, I assured the team we were fine, that we needed to pay attention, and that we just needed to focus on the fundamentals and the basics for the rest of the game. In a calm tone, I said, *Brittany, just pivot when you get in trouble. Calm down and have confidence that your teammates will be available for you when you feel pressure and discomfort. You work on this every day at practice.*

I looked at the whole team and said, *If anyone on this team cannot pivot against our competition tonight, you will not play. You will sit on the bench next to me very quickly.* I looked up and scanned the faces of my team. Then I looked at Brittany and asked, *You got this?* Brittany looked determined and responded, *Yes Coach!* The horn sounded to end the timeout and everyone high-fived and headed back out to battle our Big Ten opponent. The game was close and there was no room for more self-inflicted errors.

Adapting and Thriving

When you turn the ball over in sports, you lose a possession and it puts you back on your heels and on defense, giving your competition the opportunity to score again. The ability to pivot keeps you on offense, in control of the game, mastering the basics and ready for the unknown.

Mastering the pivot move is as critical in business as it is in sports. Sure, people in the business world may tire of hearing the word "pivot". Some feel it is overused, bankrupted, annoying, and dizzying. Guess what? My players felt the same way! They were tired of hearing me say "pivot" in practice and games, over and over and over. But I continued to reinforce the fundamental skill of adaptability to help them be more successful when they mastered it.

Just as it was important to gain comfort pivoting during chaos and pressure in a game, it is critical for people in business. If players cannot perform a pivot, in any position on the floor, they may not get recruited (hired) or they may be watching the game from the bench (fired). If they have not mastered how to pivot and cannot perform under pressure, they would be required to spend extra time in the gym on their own time to develop this skill. In the business world, lack of adaptability may result in lost individual opportunities, lost customers, lack of competitive gains, and even ethical or legal issues.

> *In the business world, an inability to pivot may result in lost individual opportunities, lost customers, lack of competitive gains, and even ethical or legal issues.*

Business and sports pivots are similar. As your leader, you would tire of hearing the word pivot from me, because I would expect everyone to be able to pivot within seconds. One never knows when you will need to adjust on the fly. In business, a rigid strategy may limit organizational success when conditions shift and strategy remains static. During a prospective client meeting, listening to and adjusting to customer needs and expectations— sometimes even unspoken—requires agility. Team members often shift responsibilities, taking up slack or filling a need another team member cannot fulfill, requiring adjustment of resources and capabilities. When you are playing against the best teams and coaches, you must be able to adjust immediately. Often, Plans A, B, and C will not work, and you and your team must pivot without showing panic and fear in the middle of a game. The world's best organizations face significant crooked rims and know agility and adaptability are keys to sustained success.

Elite athletes train to perform at a high level with calm under pressure. If a "corporate athlete" lacks training and preparation to pivot comfortably, individuals may derail under stress, displaying panic and fear. This action automatically hijacks the amygdala in the frontal cortex of the brain, resulting in a fight or flight situation. This condition strikes elite athletes, coaches, and business leaders, underscoring our responsibility to practice and to train our minds to navigate through stress, panic, fear, and anxiety. If you are ready and willing, you must master skills to manage stress and pressure as these can derail the unprepared.

Have you made a presentation, a hire, or a strategy that did not go according to the plan? Individuals, teams, and organizations who have prepared for worst-case scenarios will be able to pivot in the heat of the moment, with confidence. Each year I had a new team just as some of you have new teams every few months, and every year I knew we would face chaos and stress on the floor. You should expect the same in the business world, even if it looks a little different. To experience Final Four moments requires years of training, development, and practice to pivot when the plan loses its footing.

We will face many challenges and setbacks throughout our lives, and we must strive not to get rattled or to choke, but to pivot with grace. We all want those players on our teams who, during the most challenging times and situations, raise their hand and say, *Coach, I am ready when my number is called!* or *Coach, put me in!* or *Coach, I want the ball!* This mindset during times of crisis builds deeper trust and separates the good from the elite.

Changing With the Game

Change happens at a rapid pace and accelerates daily—some would say hourly. Unfortunately, change comes with a stigma, as if we are weary to accept the reality of the phrase, *The only constant is change.* Constant change has numbed us and, in some cases, caused us to resist either explicitly or subconsciously. To remove the stigma of fear and stress resulting from change and disruption, as well as hearing "we need to pivot again", we must boost our approach and messages. It is critical to master communication, transparency, and vulnerability during times of uncertainty to achieve buy-in and alignment.

People need to and want to understand the *why* before the *how.* In fact, many leaders and team members prefer to understand only the purpose (why) and then to define their own methods (how) without detailed instruction. You may hear the oft-used term *empowerment*, which captures the concept well: define the goal, set out the boundaries, and then give team members the freedom to accomplish the goal. Or as General George S. Patton famously said, "Never tell people how to do things. Tell them what to do and they will surprise you with their ingenuity."

Clear and transparent communication reduces confusion and mistrust and will result in quicker results. Reframing our messages is important to develop our thoughts and to lead others. Flipping the script and using positive psychology in our approach helps others embrace and thrive in chaos. Reframing a message and communicating it positively sets an opportunistic tone, and not a problematic situation that produces eye-rolling and thinking, *Here we go again.*

Over the past few years, what have been your biggest takeaways, personally and professionally? The recent events over the last 5 years, and even more so this past year, elevate our concern about how best to navigate our lives moving forward. The fact is, as we think about what we will do, we are living this future already. To achieve success now and in the next three to five years, we must embrace and be comfortable with constant change and evolve our skillsets accordingly.

It is critical to continue to increase our investment in a performance strategy and in methods to manage development and growth for ourselves and our team. Individuals must prepare to take on greater responsibility and to reinvent themselves through lifelong learning. When we think of the future in business, we should ask:

What will our industry look like?
What is the future of work?
What talent will we need?
What biases do we have that may lead to blind spots?
What value will we bring to all stakeholders, internally and externally?

Like organizations and individuals, Coaches also must continue to evolve and understand that past performance is no guarantee of future success. Our behavior as leaders, communication, motivational tactics, culture of fear and emotional abuse, expectations, people, technology, emotional intelligence—all these elements of how we play the game and show up have changed.

Coaches do not run the same plays or systems they did 5, 10, or 15 years ago. If leaders as coaches do not continue to evolve and to bring value to every stakeholder internally and externally, they will have short tenures. As the workplace continues to evolve, developing high emotional intelligence is both necessary and expected. Much of our success in business hinges on our ability to lead with a high level of people (human) skills and to build relationships.

Evolving as Leaders

In many ways, the pandemic has compressed time like an accordion, compelling us to reimagine and to implement business and personal strategies and skills needed to move forward. Even without a major crisis—global, local, or personal—we all must prove continually that we can pivot to evolve as conditions around us change. What may have worked in the past is not a guarantee, now or in the future. The rules of past engagement no longer exist. The old ways of leading and motivating must ride the tide of change as we experience the churn of unchartered waters, which requires navigating an uncharted course of leadership.

One thing we know for sure is that individual and organizational resilience is the top skill, theme and challenge globally. Resilience is the key attribute required to demonstrate emotional strength, courage, and responsiveness during the most trying times. The people we surround ourselves with matter, so make sure they are comfortable working in an ambiguous environment and thrive on change. When resilience is called on, such people will step up and perform.

Four general competencies required of leaders, who seek to perform at an exceptional level of competency, are authenticity, coaching, purpose, and innovation. Organizational leaders need to know their purpose and articulate a clear vision. Even the most on-point leaders do not have, and will not have, all the answers—they must be authentic in enlisting others to solve problems. Asking the right questions and having the right team are critically important. In a coaching environment, emotional intelligence (EQ) continues to be essential, particularly in bolstering a leader's ability to engage and to inspire team members to follow a new vision. In today's highly digital and virtual world, this high-touch, human-centered competency is critical to connect with team members, customers, and all stakeholders. How we make decisions, communicate, demonstrate our resilience, and lead as coaches are expectations that are at a high premium.

> *If leaders as coaches do not continue to evolve and to bring value to every stakeholder internally and externally, they will have short tenures.*

We must also change the way we think and focus, moving from tactical thinking to strategic leadership. Many leaders (and team members) actually enjoy the less demanding elements of their roles. Tactical, tangible tasks are easy to cross it off the list, do not take much focus or energy, and give us a sense of accomplishment. It takes time to adapt to a new-level position by tackling more creative, strategic, higher-value thinking. Remember how tired you felt after that last one-day workshop where you used your brain, worked your way through thinking and problem-solving exercises, and communicated and collaborated with others all day? Most people are not trained for or ready to do that in one day, let alone every day in their jobs. But our evolving world values strategic leadership and organizations must differentiate themselves.

Many individuals and organizations are also pivoting teams to work cross-functionally. The ability to influence others across a matrixed organization with senior leadership, peers, and middle management represents a skill that many of my clients discuss in our meetings. Engaging, integrating, and building relationships across a broader matrix with many stakeholders to reach performance goals differs significantly from the typical, historical hierarchy and reporting.

We also are experiencing a workforce characterized by a significant gap between older and younger workers; people are working later in life, having multiple careers, and collaborating with five generations in the workplace for the first time in history. The extremes of generations in the workplace have an impact on how flexible an organization's culture needs to be. The changing landscape means we need to adapt and to develop our own skills and those of our teams if we are to remain competitive and to take advantage of new opportunities. In addition to the skills that future leaders will themselves require, they also need to level up the surrounding talent in the organization to help them meet the challenges of tomorrow.

Diverse teams and inclusive cultures offer a way to elevate our individual and organizational competitiveness. This is vital for business success now and in the future. A study by *Forbes* found that inclusive teams make better business decisions 87% of the time, with diverse teams delivering 60% better results. As our digital, virtual world continues to emphasize seamless communication and rapid results, it will be increasingly important for organizations to build inclusive cultures and a diverse workforce to mirror their consumer base and to enable them to innovate. A diverse workforce that does not make people feel included and allow them to speak up and be themselves at work, will not reap the benefits of the workforce's unique perspectives and skills. Leadership teams should also mirror the consumer base of the business, so they can walk in their customers' shoes.

The worldwide remote work style, now and moving forward, challenges our resilience as it requires us to "always be on", with a high focus on health and well-being. Before the pandemic, two-thirds of workers experienced burnout in the workplace, according to job search site Monster.com. Stress and financial anxiety are high, yet workers are not taking enough time off to recharge, fearing they could be in the next layoff if they do not work hard enough. Fear and stress take a toll on our overall physical, mental, and emotional health. In a remote workplace, a top stressor involves juggling work and home life. Kids are stuck at home, experiencing remote learning for the first time, while both spouses often work from home in makeshift offices as they struggle to keep the family together. When these families fear that one spouse may get laid off or take a salary cut, the level of stress in the home impacts the resilience, health, and well-being of everyone under the roof.

In a truly inclusive culture, organizations understand that the greatest talent could be anywhere in the world. Organizations benefit from nurturing a culture and building systems that decentralize control, encourage people to constantly learn and evolve, and empower people to take charge and embrace change. Leadership now and in the near future must design a strategy and implement a game plan for performance management, from picking the right people to ensuring they perform at their best.

Why is it that some people, when faced with adversity, are forced to defend themselves against further onslaughts and build barriers, while others transform it into a challenge and meet it head on? We are more resilient than we give ourselves credit for; human beings are equipped to deal with most of what life throws at us. But, in the absence of learning, developing, and refining our human skills, many people lack the self-confidence to use these underdeveloped skills when we need them the most.

Our self-belief and perception of chaos and stress could be the single most important factors in a moment of adversity and over time. A high level and a full bucket of resilience fosters our overall well-being and happiness. Strengthening and sustaining it takes intentional self-care. Many of us resist change and we rely on doing what we know works. The current health crisis, hampered by an over-extended global supply chain and under-supported health care providers, offers a real-time example of the benefits for embracing new ways of thinking and behaving. And, it provides a testing ground for resilience—globally, nationally, locally, and in each of us as individuals.

* * *

The practice of pivoting enables leaders to mobilize people, resources, technologies, organizations, and communities more effectively. A pivot that leverages resources, processes, people, systems, and technology in a coordinated manner could lead to the development of an innovative workforce, responsive supply chain, effective disaster recovery, and a valuable crisis management plan for use today and in the future. With the discipline of continuous improvement, effective leaders and their teams can pivot to mobilize essential workers across the organization or enterprise to execute business strategy and to take care of each other and their customers.

Working with clients, I have seen how an inability to pivot and to adapt reveals a large gap and need for understanding. An ability to pivot is not an "if", but a "when" and "where"—if it happens rapidly enough. To be innovative through disruption and to confront chaos, to reframe adversity into opportunity, we must learn new moves and master the basics of the pivot move, with confidence.

MASTER YOUR MINDSET: Your Pivot

✦ What current or expected conditions in your life or at work may require a pivot?

✦ What barriers—tangible and intangible— keep you and your team members from pivoting?

✦ How are you building and cultivating diversity and a culture of inclusiveness?

8

Mastering Your Mindset

"Champions aren't made in gyms. Champions are made from something they have deep inside them—a desire, a dream, a vision. They have to have the skill. And the will. But the will must be stronger than the skill."

–MUHAMMAD ALI–

In today's world it is paramount that we understand the need to take control of our own self-care. It has become our primary focus in many ways. Start by envisioning what self-care looks and feels like—physically, emotionally, and mentally. This is our launch pad to begin putting our discipline, tools, strategies, and resources in order, giving us the best chance to accomplish everything on our full plates.

Mindset Matters

To sustain and reach peak performance, we must accept responsibility to control our primary care holistically from the inside out. Our personal choices anchored by our individual beliefs shape the level of commitment we make to live a life of limitless resilience and possibility.

Does mindset matter? Building a resilient mindset and then learning to master it are the first steps in strengthening resilience. A healthy and strong mindset sets us on a course to achieve the hopes, dreams, aspirations, and goals that we set for ourselves. Living life and getting through difficult times takes sheer grit and hope. In many situations, our confidence, self-regard, and self-talk fuel a high level of performance, making us feel unstoppable. In those moments, we enter our zone. Daily routines and rituals provide consistency, structure, and safety in uncertain times.

Elite athletes develop and nurture a strong sense of self in order to perform at elite levels. Reaching this point in their overall development creates a competitive advantage. Many of us have not been equipped with the same level of training, experience, or coaching to master our mindset at an elite level. If we commit, we can reshape the way we think from the inside out. *What possible shifts or adjustments do you need to take steps forward?*

Private Conversations

Our external communication allows us to form deep relationships, build trust, and connect in complex environments. However, our internal dialogue shapes our perception and drives how we show up in life, pushing us forward or holding us back. When we are alone, our private, intimate, internal conversations provide a running dialogue and soundtrack to our lives. We can shape our own beliefs about ourselves, either positive or negative, and we can choose to have an amazing impact on ourselves. Creating a positive conversation in our own heads can motivate, reassure, and build strength and self-confidence. There are many times I have given myself a pep-talk before a game or presentation. It would go like this:

You got this. You are going to go out there and knock it out of the park. You are going to dominate tonight and people will be cheering you on. If you make a mistake—and it will happen—smile and move on quickly like nothing happened. No one will be able to tell and they do not care. You will inspire others and make a difference that impacts their lives. You were born for this. You have prepared your whole life for moments like this. You are going to be amazing. I CAN. I WILL. I AM.

There are many self-affirming and effective messages you can adopt; be true to yourself and own your mindset. Unfortunately, many of us entertain private conversations with deflating, paralyzing, and derailing words and thoughts. Focusing on negative thoughts can lead to decreased motivation, feed anxiety and depression, and give rise to feelings of hopelessness. When these self-defeating conversations get out of hand they can take over, becoming destructive and even leading to mental health issues. Despite their elite level, this dilemma haunted many of my players and limited their performance and overall success. When negativity hijacked their mentality, they lost confidence in their physical abilities and in their decision-making, leading to missed shots, turnovers, and mistakes in offensive and defensive assignments. And they ended up sitting next to me.

This type of toxic thinking must get corrected. The good news is that we can change our mindset and create the private conversations we want. I used positive psychology, relaxation techniques, or tactics unique to each player. Many times, when performance lapsed, it is not the mechanics or the skill, it is the mental or emotional capabilities of that individual. This is a constant reminder that we are all works-in-progress. When we think we have arrived at the top, beware of celebrating your intelligence or talents instead of developing them. We all must continue to have a passion for learning rather than a hunger for approval.

Elite athletes learn the hard way through failure throughout their careers. We all have wasted time and energy trying to prove our greatness over and over, rather than focusing on getting better every day. The lucky among us learn this lesson early in our careers through experiences that emphasize failure and learning. The best coaches and the best teammates hold us accountable and help us keep our edge in these times.

To support your efforts in mastering your mindset, you must surround yourself with partners and friends who will not just tell you how wonderful you are but will challenge you to grow and to get better. Seek out experiences that will expand your comfort zone and people who will stretch you. Develop a mindset and passion for challenging yourself and sticking to it, even if it is not going well. This is how we grow and master our mindset, allowing us to thrive during some of the most difficult times in our lives.

> *Surround yourself with partners and friends who will not just tell you how wonderful you are but will tell you the truth and challenge you to grow and to get better.*

Many athletes—and leaders in the workplace—may not have the level of experience, maturity, or perspective to get themselves out of slumps. Coaches and business leaders see players and employees beating themselves up all the time. As we identify the core drivers of our mindset, we learn how to reprogram our mentality to become elite, holistically. Through effort and self-challenge, we focus on our emotional and mental capacity and learn to reframe negative, destructive, and unproductive thoughts. Replacing these thoughts with positive self-talk, affirming beliefs, and visualization of past experiences can help reprogram our mindset.

As a coach, I utilize an appreciative inquiry approach that draws from positive psychology and storytelling. Appreciative inquiry is a strengths-based, positive approach to individual growth, leadership development, and organizational change. I leverage this approach with my clients often to align their strengths rather than to enable their weaknesses. This approach helps individuals through rough patches, battling a crisis of confidence, and teaches them to move on quickly from failure.

Some leaders and coaches take a different approach and focus on the weaknesses and problems that surface; they are problem-centric. I ask them to think back to a time, a past experience, when they were performing at their peak. I ask them to relate how they felt and what they did to reach that level of performance. As they describe it, they reclaim this successful past experience and relive it, recognizing the elements of their peak performance mentality. Bringing context to their story-telling, I then ask my clients to identify and to integrate the positive elements to address their present and future paths forward. Appreciative inquiry and other positive psychology approaches serve to reprogram our mindset with a can-do attitude and changes behavior necessary to overcome any current adversity or performance slump.

Getting the Mental Edge

Mike was the top producer in his technology sales organization for many years. His work ethic, drive, and can-do attitude gave him a successful sales foundation. Mike worked hard to build relationships and trust with his customers and he embraced and mastered change and disruption that had become the norm in big tech industries. He was comfortable pivoting and his coworkers and clients described him as unflappable.

Mike was an integral part of many new product launches, sales strategy, leadership changes, and market shifts. Because of his track record, his organization called his number to step into a senior leadership role during the pandemic. He was asked to lead the entire sales organization and to develop a strategic plan and processes that would drive sales in the wake of the pandemic, social unrest, and a wary economy. Mike admitted that his success and now this new role during an unprecedented time came with a personal price tag. His success in sales and the commitment it required put a lot of pressure and stress on his personal life. Now, as he accepted even greater responsibility, he realized he had lost control and he needed to pause, take a step back, and rebuild his inner strength and resilience.

Mike's inner voice questioned his "why" and challenged him to assess what he was doing. He was unsure if he was good enough for this new role, he was working longer hours, and his relationships began to show all the warning signs of stress. He began to doubt if he could do this job and if he had the mental energy to lead during a crisis. His resilience and inner strength were being tested and it was impacting his self-belief. Mike reached out for help and said that he needed a coach to help him during his challenging times.

I worked with Mike for a year and we designed a road map to rebuild his inner strength and resilience. He worked hard to set and to celebrate small, achievable goals; he increased his confidence in his new role, learned to delegate, and found a little balance in his life. Mike worked hard to master his mindset and was determined to rise above the challenges and excel. Rebuilding his inner strength, Mike found success in his new role and achieved the balance he needed.

Achieving Self-Awareness

After we decide that we need to master our own mindset, we find that self-awareness holds the secret to boost our inner strength. Self-awareness pushes us to know ourselves in context of the unexpected challenges that life brings; it helps us identify what to expect from ourselves and also to recognize the one thing we can control—our response. Observing what is going on around us solidifies the critical need for a high level of self-awareness. We experience change in so many ways, constantly and consistently. Today, global conditions no longer guarantee the safety and security we desire in our lives. In order to thrive in our ever-changing world, we need to develop one of the most important dimensions of leadership: becoming our authentic selves and building our reserves of inner strength.

Resilience and inner strength help us get back up when we have been knocked down. We empower ourselves when we dust ourselves off and get back into the game. Individuals with inner strength possess the mental and emotional skills to confront the challenges that life brings. Developing our self-awareness muscle allows us to respond rather than react to adversity and stress, embracing the opportunity to overcome rather than succumb to challenges. It is motivating to know that we can increase our inner strength and self-awareness with practice. Today's leaders have experienced considerable pressure from pivoting their lives and leadership to combat the multiple crooked rim crises we all face today. Whether we face daily life difficulties or global crises, developing a keen sense of awareness, trusting ourselves, and surrounding ourselves with positive people gives us the fuel to push forward. Our inner strength relates directly to our outer strength.

It is not easy to navigate our way out of being bogged down from the weight of discouragement, fear, and uncertainty. By becoming more self-aware and noticing our triggers and reactions—words, sights, sounds, emotions, feelings, situations, circumstances, and even people—we can gain confidence in our ability to respond appropriately and professionally. Our future generation watches and learns from us, both the good and the bad.

> *Developing our self-awareness muscle allows us to respond rather than react to adversity and stress, embracing the opportunity to overcome rather than succumb to challenges.*

Our ability to better understand ourselves and to control our impulses and reactions is a lifelong journey. Understanding the underlying reasons for triggers and resistance to change requires a high level of self-awareness. Many people resist and push back because they fear they may look incompetent and feel insecure; ultimately, they experience an imposter syndrome, doubting their skills, talents, and capabilities and hiding from being exposed as a fraud. However, we can convert this vulnerability into power and create goals to learn new skills that enable our success.

The 2020 Presidential election offered an opportunity to practice our emotional control and reactions. As the campaign unfolded and policies, values, and behaviors rose to the forefront, we questioned the basis of our emotional responses to our family members and friends who may have different priorities, beliefs, or understandings. Our emotional reactions often reflect our interpretations and the stories that we convince ourselves are true.

Our stories are often subconscious and frequently depart from reality. Ask yourself, *What is my primary reason for feeling this way? Am I reacting from fear, frustration, or anger instead of responding with patience, consideration, and thoughtfulness?* Once you identify the emotion, ask yourself, *What is this really about? What do I believe to be true that is making me feel this way?* To identify and manage our emotions and behaviors effectively, we need to ask ourselves these types of questions. This helps to illuminate the stories that drive our emotions, influence our perceptions, and affect our behaviors.

Becoming an Emotional Master-Athlete

Developing and strengthening self-awareness was critical in the overall development of my players. It was as important as dribbling, defending, shooting, and playing the game. Self-awareness is key in our journeys to reach the next level and think and react like the world's best.

One of the players I had the privilege to coach was an All-American and one of the top players in the nation. Most of the time, she showcased a jaw-dropping skillset and physical abilities on the court. However, this player had not developed and did not understand the importance of self-awareness and a lack of control over her behavior derailed her on many occasions. All four holistic skills; physical, mental, emotional, and purpose, must be developed, practiced, and honed. When she did not develop all four of these skills, she earned many technical fouls, fouled out of games, and got derailed on the court in front of thousands of fans on national television. She said things she regretted to her teammates and coaches and mentally took herself out of games because of the stress, pressure, and events that happened on the court.

This player also had a low competency in her mental strength and her emotional capacity that did not support consistent or sustainable performance. Negative emotions ignited her energy—but it drove her performance down instead of up. Over time, those feelings and actions became toxic and crippled her performance and, ultimately, hurt the team. When she experienced anxiousness, fear, insecurity, and high expectations, she withdrew from the team and would take a "backseat" in the middle of a game. When she reached this point, she was likely to choke in competition and anger and frustration crippled her capacity to stay confident, calm, and in control.

I intervened with this star player and provided tools, strategies, and training to help her develop the mental and emotional skills needed to be successful in the moment and to support her opportunity for a long professional career. She was stubborn initially, stuck in her ways, with a fixed mindset and closed-minded; at the time, I thought that she may have an inability to change. In the end, it took building a deep trust in each other to work through strengthening her mental and emotional skills and, after a couple of years, the self-limiting emotions and behavior tapered off. She strengthened these skills and performed and responded to adversity like an All-American. At the end of her college career, she became the top draft pick in the WNBA draft.

The impact of self-awareness on business performance is more nuanced but no less significant. Self-awareness can be career enriching or career ending for anyone. Whether you are a frontline employee, middle management, or a seasoned executive, achieving self-awareness is a critical step before you can begin a journey of self-improvement. Most of us personally experience the downside if we lack this skill or we have observed the self-limiting issues of others many times. The result is usually not in that individual's favor, unless a coach helps you take this on like I did with my number one draft pick. You decide: *Will you continue to be part of your problem or choose to be part of your solution?*

Emerging From Within

We have never faced as much pressure as we do today. As we navigate the evolving global crisis, expectations are sky high. Stakeholders call for growth, broader strategies, resilience, and sustainable value. For purpose-led organizations, the global crisis represents a defining moment. Crystal-clear priorities will be key to set future-focused goals and people will continue to be the critical asset in any organization.

The connection between happiness at work and overall life satisfaction, employee happiness, and workforce well-being and resilience can make a difference in overall health and wellness—and individual and organizational performance. The research clearly demonstrates the relationship between investment in employee development and turnover/retention, sick days, employee engagement, customer experience, and other key performance indicators that indicate organizational success. Strategies to implement health and wellness strategies in your life, for your team, and across the organization must be a compelling priority.

To get started, first make a commitment to master your own mindset. After you choose to go all in, the investment you make to expand your self-awareness calls on your internal resources. As we commit to our mindset and self-awareness, we will begin to see challenges and opportunities differently, make better decisions for our personal and professional lives, and connect with our true and authentic selves. Looking inward takes courage and it will expose our vulnerabilities. *Are you interested in creating new opportunities and becoming the best version of yourself?* If the answer is "yes", then muster the courage and dig deeply; the level of effort you put in will dictate the level of return you get back.

Hopes and dreams require acting on aspirations by putting plans into action. *How else would they come true?* Peak performers act decisively and live in the moment while holding a vivid vision for what is possible. Their vison is clearly etched in their minds. Yet even a peak performer can start to see their life going downhill quickly; one thing after another can cause life events to become a runaway train. Think for a moment about where you are today and your own experience, then think about those around you. The ripple effect from the pandemic, social injustice, and an economic crisis have induced a mental health crisis that affects all of us, those at the peak and those on the slopes climbing up. It is up to each of us to look within and take action to improve our overall well-being.

* * *

Many of us have faced challenges: job loss, stress and anxiety, remote work, return to work uncertainties, workplace safety risks, sleep disturbances, weight loss/gain, alcohol use/abuse, drug use/addiction, depression, suicide, isolation, climate change, school closing/reopening, daycare instability, teacher safety concerns, healthcare and essential worker strain, and a tumultuous Presidential election. Every day raises threats to our resilience, and we must all understand that self-care should be our primary objective moving forward. We have control and must be on point for our own health and overall well-being.

When we choose to master our mindset and strengthen self-awareness, we accept full responsibility for and ownership of our self-care. Our lives are meant to be abundant and we have the ability and the internal resources to strengthen our resilience to live, lead, and perform limitlessly.

MASTER YOUR MINDSET: Your Mental Muscle

✦ What shifts or adjustments do you need to master your mindset?

✦ How will you increase your self-awareness?

✦ What is your level of commitment to self-care in all four competencies, and what actions will you take to elevate them?

PART 3

THE NEXT LEVEL

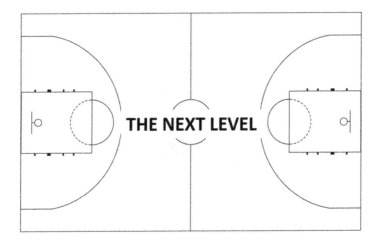

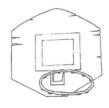

9

The Elite Athlete Within

"There are victories of the soul and spirit.
Sometimes, even if you lose, you win."
–ELIE WIESEL–

Every athlete has a coach; every championship team has a great coach. Elite athletes want to play for the best coaches. Professional athletes like LeBron James and Serena Williams have a stable of coaches to help them be the best in many ways, from strength and flexibility to mental performance to nutrition and sport-specific techniques. Elite athletes also want to play for the best teams and organizations. They want to be surrounded by the best teammates who are driven, have a tremendous work ethic, display a team-first attitude, and demonstrate selfless and positive attitudes. *Would this be a dream come true in the business world?*

The Elite Athlete

Coaches and athletes understand what it takes to be elite—to be a pro and to win. They implement strategies to ensure a sustained career and focus on what it takes to perform at their peak every single day. The "best of the best" are fortunate to have careers that could last up to 15 years or more in the pros, if they are lucky and do everything right. Depending on the sport, their training and focus on well-being, they understand that their development starts from the inside out. Elite athletes who wish to sustain long careers, take a holistic approach to support and maintain high performance and longevity.

As I look back on my farm upbringing, the crooked rim, and the bright lights in The Barn, I realize I had been training my whole life in this multilevel way. I learned throughout my journey what I needed to do and how to pivot to sustain high performance daily in the face of increasing stress, pressure, and unrealistic expectations in a fast-paced environment of constant change.

Managing performance and achieving results for talented coaches, athletes, and teams who seek greatness does not require magic. It requires nothing more than focusing on the aspects of an elite athlete and not one of these elements are more important than another. The mistake that most make is not developing and training in all facets to reach an optimal state; typically, an athlete, and most head coaches and leaders today, overlook the emotional and mental training necessary to support their performance and the expectations that come with the position. If they do not train in and develop each of these four key areas, they hinder their performance and will experience a short tenure.

An athlete's competitive season has clear definition, and they compete about four or five hours a day. They also have an off-season to recover and recharge; great athletes know how to maximize the benefits of this time. This recovery-recharge time is as important, if not more, than their physical training and season. The best professional athletes' careers can last until they are around 35 years old, when they are towards the end of their prime and in their highest earning years. Of course, there also outlier athletes like Tom Brady, Sue Bird, and Drew Brees, still performing at a high level in their forties through a disciplined focus on all four aspects of performance.

Elite coaches and athletes are wired differently than the average person. They are extremely competitive, Type A, and driven with a mindset to achieve the impossible. In sports, to achieve the impossible, one does not even entertain a self-limiting mindset or belief. The parallels are striking when comparing sports and the business world. In both arenas, elite performers are not born—they are developed. True, the elite athlete has some innate natural abilities, and so do many senior executives who need to be able to think strategically and coach people to perform and get results at a high level. With the competition breathing down their neck, the expectations of high performance and results are the same for elite athletes and business people: excel and win.

Very quickly I recognized the vast difference in talent in the business world; many organizations or teams do not develop bench strength and have ineffective performance management approaches. Between the sports and business worlds, approaches differ greatly for how the best continue to get better in achieving individual and organizational excellence. Sports organizations focus on excellence every day and they invest in it. In the business world, very few organizations know where to begin and how to achieve and sustain excellence. And when they do make an investment, it is for an hour- or day-long training workshop, or maybe a several-day event. The business world typically looks at human performance development as an event and not a process.

If you want to perform at an optimal level, managing stress and pressure at a rapid pace requires a whole-person approach in the game of life. My players wanted to be the best and now my clients want to be the best and sustain it. Getting there takes having a plan, an intentional focus, goals, and a game plan. Taking a holistic approach is not optional anymore. If we focus on or perform well in only one or two of the performance aspects, we would probably feel unfulfilled and frustrated; we will also miss or get overlooked for opportunities. Continuous growth and learning to reinvent and level up our capabilities and skillset strengthens our resilience, mindset, confidence, and overall performance.

The best athletes and executives spend countless hours preparing. They stretch themselves and they endure countless failures. Disruptive forces stare us in the face daily; if we want to be elite performers, we must embrace all four competencies to flourish. We fail to realize that the corporate athlete "competes" 10 to 12 hours a day, their jobs are not seasonal, and their careers span 40 years. Most businesses lack a focus on training and development in each of these areas—to survive what life constantly throws at us, in today's environment, requires a major mental and behavioral reset. *This may sound straightforward, but where do you begin?*

In comparison to the elite athlete, the corporate athlete often does not have a coach, a team coach, or even teammates who are talented or good team players. Many leadership teams are not high functioning or even rowing in the same direction. Corporate athletes are also wired differently; many do not take training seriously or understand that a holistic approach may produce transformational results. A focus on physical health, mental strength, emotional capacity, and purposeful work will allow the corporate athlete to thrive under pressure and excel when the heat is on.

> *Disruptive forces stare us in the face daily; if we want to be elite performers, we must develop and master our physical, mental, emotional, and purpose elements to flourish.*

An inability to step up and to embrace chaos and a crisis will expose anyone quickly, particularly when others need us most. High-stress situations and constant pressure control our behaviors and impulses when we are under fire. Managing adversity in the moment like a pro is an elite trait we all should aspire to develop. If this is something you are interested in pursuing and mastering, make a choice and then commit passionately to you own growth and self-improvement. It is worth the effort and price.

Sports and business today share many similarities. Sports have become a business and a machine, and the best players keep getting better because they are expected to win consistently. Today's business environment features significantly higher levels of urgency and complexity than in years' past. Business and executive coaches must bring value to their clients to reach new levels of performance and to ensure success during unprecedented times. Business leaders must elevate their attention on human performance management to differentiate from the competition and to address the diverse demands and retention in the workplace. The individuals and teams—in sports and business—with the best chance of sustained success embrace high-stress situations and have developed high levels of resilience in the four performance areas.

Over my career as a basketball coach, expectations continued to shift, the speed of change accelerated, and the stress mounted every year. The collegiate athletics arms race gained momentum during my tenure and shows no signs of slowing today. College sports programs invest more and more to build the biggest, most lavish facilities. According to a *USA Today* September 23, 2020, article, College coaches were the highest-paid public employees in all but 10 states. The more money that is invested, the higher the expectations. The collegiate sports industry advanced quickly, the players evolved, the game changed, and so does leadership.

These conditions differ little from what we experience now in the business world. The most successful companies invest in technology, product development, marketing, consultants who are experts, and the development of their people. The "haves" continue to separate their organizations from the "have-nots", driving greater revenue and margins and integrating their products and services into our daily lives seamlessly. As crisis and uncertainty increased in our world, we observe how many successful leaders stepped up, rose to the occasion, and flourished. Unfortunately, we have seen many leaders, public and private, crash and burn from a lack of courage, leadership, preparedness, and stress management. These leaders failed to set themselves up to handle a crisis before it happened.

Emotional intelligence and resilience correlate strongly with our own optimal performance. As a basketball coach, I learned this holistic approach for my optimal development as I was expected to represent the best. This approach also became part of our team culture, values, training, and tradition in order for my players and coaches to perform—and win—at the elite Big Ten level. The expectations did not change from year after year; the stakes just continued to get higher.

Now, as a senior executive coach, my clients desire and can relate to this approach. For each client, mastering their mindset and the approach they take is exactly what I mastered myself on the court and also with my own executive coach. There is a methodology and approach to experience this transformation. For those seeking sustainable success, such an approach is not optional; there are more demands, higher expectations, and deeper complexities today in the workplace. Executives and their employees all seek high levels of performance as "corporate athletes", a term coined by Jim Loehr and Tony Schwartz in a 2001 *Harvard Business Review* article.

The journey to fulfilment and success as a corporate athlete first means stepping up to the plate. Our own mindset propels us forward or sabotages our progress. Mastering our mindset and developing self-awareness gets us out of the batter's box and heading to first base. Then, developing a growth mindset will take us to new heights as we round the bases. Developing high-performing teams and exceeding results, under pressure and in the middle of chaos, cannot be learned in a class. Leadership during a time of crisis requires an ability to win the hearts and minds of people. This is true leadership and a skill that always has come natural to me in my leadership roles.

Building trust quickly and winning the hearts and the minds of my corporate athletes was a seamless, natural transition for me. As I refined my niche of working with individuals leading people and teams, the importance of a holistic approach to all aspects of our lives was reinforced. I learned that performance outcomes extend beyond business results and include positive or negative effects on our physical, mental, and emotional health. Elite athletes commit to being elite with just one tactic: they go all in.

Have you ever considered yourself a corporate athlete, ready to go all in? You should . . . because you are expected to perform like one every day. The vision and goals to perform and to compete on a daily basis in your role requires all the elements of elite athletic competition: grit, hard work, focus, time management, resilience, determination, mental strength, and emotional control. Driven and caring executives can relate to the training that athletes undertake to reach peak performance and the teamwork illustrated by great teams. Think of your day at work as an athletic performance, where your preparation and execution determine your success. Then put in the work to master your mindset to sustain enhanced health, peak performance, and happiness.

Our lives, careers, and experiences do not always turn out the way we drew them up. We have our dreams, but the X's and O's and the plays we perfectly planned out for our lives and careers never cooperate. After years of coaching, training, and working with some of the best players and leaders in the world, I have rooted my approach as a master executive coach and leadership consultant in developing the complete and whole person, leader, executive, and team—just as I did when developing the whole student-athlete as a coach. The goal and focus for my players were to develop and to reach their full potential as a whole person. This approach and mindset serve as the main goal for my clients today.

Physical Health Matters

Our body is the most important instrument we will ever learn to play. In sports, physical conditioning, exercise, nutrition, and sleep clearly are critical to an elite athlete's performance. Our body is our main energy source and our foundation for everything we do—mentally, emotionally, and physically. Physical activity and exercise support a healthy body, preventing illness, injury, and potential life-threatening health issues. With the level of stress, pressure, change, and crisis many senior executives (and all of us) face daily, taking care of our physical health helps us be the best for ourselves and others and produces important physiological and mental health outcomes. Because we push ourselves so hard every day, a lack of fitness affects our emotions, behaviors, and decision-making and undermines our performance.

An inactive, sedentary lifestyle puts individuals at risk for health issues. Inactivity may cause cardiovascular disease, Type 2 diabetes, high blood pressure, high cholesterol, and a host of physical and mental impacts. I have worked with clients who take more medications than they want to admit. Their excuse? They did not have time in their day for themselves. Their stress level, depression, anxiety, work and family expectations left them unable to find the time for themselves. Yes, these factors take a toll on the best of us, yet we must elevate our physical health to be a top priority. Many of my clients set performance goals to ensure they focus on their health and well-being. Controlling this part of one's life almost guarantees higher satisfaction, a better outlook on life, and overall happiness. Physical activity, sleep, and nutrition all play a starting role in all aspects of our life.

> *Exercise, nutrition, and sleep are critical to an elite NCAA or corporate athlete's performance. Our body is our main energy source and our foundation for everything we do mentally, emotionally, and physically.*

Emotional Wellness Mindset

Life offers opportunities for hope, ambition, and possibilities. It also presents circumstances that produce fear, negativity, frustration, and sadness. We have control to choose *how* we show up in life. As management guru Stephen R. Covey said, "Proactive people can carry their own weather with them. Whether it rains or shines makes no difference to them." Making a choice to understand who we are and to develop self-awareness becomes the difference between the good and the great. No matter our age, experience, or position at work or in life, this choice presents itself throughout our lifetime.

When we manage our thoughts, our behavior, and the narrative in our mind, we find calm, peace, and a key ingredient that supports mental toughness: positivity. The inability to manage and to control our internal climate derails us from being at our best. When elite athletes perform at their optimal level, they express confidence, demonstrate passion, feel calm, and embrace challenges. Your intentional choice to practice and to train your mind will develop the power of positivity and optimism as consistent skills.

Each day challenges us to manage our negative thoughts and emotions. Lacking the tools and strategies to manage negativity in our thoughts ultimately will cripple one's performance and, eventually, a career. This represents a growth opportunity common to men and women. When athletes feel fear, impulsivity, frustration, negativity, and anxiety, coaches must step in to help them learn how to manage their emotions, and ensuring they learn not to get too high or too low on any occasion. We teach them how to change their narrative, let go quickly and flip the script, and change the messages running through their minds.

I have seen many individuals who did not make it because they could not control their emotions, behavior, words, and body language. They were often minimized and even sometimes fired. Becoming more aware of the triggers and signals in your mind and body during stress, anxiety, and in the middle of a crisis contributes to improved performance. Along with physical skills typically part of an athlete's daily training, psychology for high performance is a major aspect coaches focus on intentionally.

Strengthening resilience and then developing mental toughness pave the path to consistent peak performance. If anger, depression, or emotional tiredness drain you, just imagine shedding these derailers to perform at your best. Developing positive emotions, relationships, and mindsets for yourself and in others results in a higher level of retention, engagement, growth, health, and inspiration.

Mental Muscle

Developing mental strength enhances our performance. Mental strength results from discipline, focus, commitment, and a determination to be more efficient, effective, and consistent. Mental strength skills need a plan and require discipline to enable better time management, delegation, focus, strategic thinking, critical thinking, and problem solving. Senior-level leaders must train their people and teams as corporate athletes to develop and to hone strong mental capacities as they continue to climb the ladder and plan for succession.

When roles and responsibilities change in business—just like on athletic teams—so does the focus and the concentrated effort required to perform effectively. For my former student-athletes, class, homework, practice, film, travel, tutors, and community service took a lot of discipline, time management, visualization and prioritization. Much of our training at the Division I level focused on managing time, practicing discipline, and juggling priorities as athletes in order to excel on and off the court. These demands placed a premium on the athlete's responsibility to manage their energy level. Being able to recover and to manage their level of stress, high expectations, workload, and competing priorities in life was an art that required focus and discipline.

Today's unique challenges and the unknown future elevate the importance of a strong mental game. The pandemic created an overwhelming level of change, chaos, and disruption in our lives and, overnight, our work and home lives changed drastically. Working from home while managing kids in virtual school, losing jobs and income, experiencing financial insecurity, and suffering from social isolation took a substantial toll on everyone. As these conditions pushed us away from our norms, the mental aspects of how we function came to the forefront. My clients worked to strengthen their focus and develop mental wellness into their daily routines to ensure their personal and professional success.

> *Today's unique challenges and the unknown future elevate the importance of a strong mental game. Developing a high level of mental strength minimizes or eliminates the feeling of spiraling out of control.*

Needless to say, most of us do not prepare for the mental onslaught we face in daily life, let alone in a global health and economic crisis. Developing a high level of mental strength minimizes or eliminates the feeling of spiraling out of control. Start by learning to manage your energy level more effectively, create balance in your life, and revive your passion. Set goals to increase mental strength, have a plan to develop the skills, and build in practice and recovery into your daily routine and you will feel more confident and productive.

Purpose at Our Core

Everyone expresses values and passion through our beliefs and actions in our lives. However, I have worked with many individuals and teams who struggle to realize and communicate a purpose and vision for themselves. *Why is it so difficult to translate our personal values into professional values?* Organizations often do not take the time to define a shared purpose and they produce a "marketing" message that does not inspire true support or action. Many tend to wait until they hit adversity, challenges, and poor team dynamics before they address the topic about why they exist and who they serve as a team and organization.

We can express our "why" easily when we are winning and everything is going well. Yet the times in our lives when we face challenges or hit rock bottom leave us stumbling along and unable to see the light at the end of the tunnel. Some may feel lost and hopeless. *So how does our purpose relate to optimal performance?* Understanding and clearly defining what that is so everyone understands why we do what we do generates inspiration, energy, and excitement by tapping into what is most important. We want to be part of something bigger than ourselves; a strong sense of purpose fulfills our need for meaning and enables us to show up as our authentic selves. Understanding and knowing our purpose strengthens our resilience and motivation.

In the 21st Century, purpose-driven organizations make a strong connection to the core with their employees and other stakeholders. According to a *Workplace Culture* report, almost nine out of ten, or 86%, of our future generation of Millennial leaders would accept a pay cut to be part of an organization whose purpose and values align with their own. By 2025, Millennials will comprise roughly 75% of the global workforce. How we connect, partner, communicate, build trust, and bring high value to all stakeholders in our ecosystem differentiates the elite organizations from the also-rans.

A company's greatest asset is its people. This is more than just a throw-away, overused consultant phrase. Look around and see if customer experience, product innovation, problem-solving, strategic accomplishment, competitive differentiation, or any other activity in your organization would continue without high-performing team members. Think about your highest- and lowest-performing teammates or departments; now, picture the high performers leaving your organization for greener pastures. Companies who fail to invest in their most talented and also in developing others fail to understand the problem.

For the companies solely focused on the numbers and business results, the train has left the station and it is likely you are experiencing issues recruiting talent, engaging team members, and retaining key performers. High performers and your future talent desire more than just money, titles, and promotions. They crave meaning, want to make an impact and difference, and seek to contribute to a purpose greater than themselves. Successful organizations create a sense of belonging and a deep connectedness that humans need, with business outcomes following closely. A sense of belonging strengthens one's resilience and connectedness in the workplace.

Identifying our legacy and working to leave a mark on this world affirms our sense of purpose. When we figure this out in our lives, it is transformational. We do not just go to work; we work to create value and meaning. We not only figure out *how* to lead; we realize *why* we want to lead. When leaders reach this inflection point, they lead with increased empathy, compassion, and authenticity. The purposeful leader becomes a coach and prepares others for success with a focus and goal to maximize their potential. Such leaders remain open and create space for collaboration and innovation. These leaders drive sustained organizational—and individual—success.

> *Identifying our legacy and working to leave*
> *a mark on this world affirms our sense of purpose.*
> *We do not just go to work, we work to*
> *create value and meaning.*

Lasting Legacy

I was one of three executive coaches that Jim, a successful CEO and owner of a family-owned business, interviewed for a coaching opportunity. Over a 12-month period, he wanted help and support in preparing for succession and transferring leadership in his company. His son Mark served as the CFO and stood next in line for the CEO position. Jim was proactive and thoughtful in setting his son up for success with executive coaching to enable a smoother transition.

My phone rang on a Friday evening. Jim wondered if I would be interested in working with him and Mark at the same time, asking "Coach, would you be able to start next week? I would like you to work with us over the next 12 months and possibly beyond as Mark transitions into the CEO role." I explained confidentiality, described my approach, onboarding, and the coaching process. I outlined how I would work with Jim to transfer leadership, help him to let go, and introduce Mark to positions and opportunities over the next 12 months to get experience and build confidence before plunging full-time into the CEO role.

Even organizations that recognize the importance of a smooth, structured leadership transition often neglect other factors that relate to the new CEO's success. Jim and I discussed his bench strength on the senior leadership team and skillsets that could fill in the gaps as roles and responsibilities shifted. I noted that Jim also would need to evaluate others' roles based on Mark's strengths, gaps, and relationships. Jim was excited, agreed that it all made sense, and recognized that my proposed approach was more comprehensive than he had envisioned—it would set up Mark, the team, and his organization up for success.

Jim started the company 40 years prior and, as the CEO and founder, he knew every customer and even their families. He had built a $500-million company and was the only salesperson. He did it all; he was the face of the company and was always an arm's length away from every vendor, client, and prospect. His pipeline was full, he was a master at cold calling, he sparked a conversation with anyone, and would light up a room as soon as he walked in. His gifts of charisma and ability to connect with others served the organization well. Jim started to understand that we could not, nor could Mark, replace those traits. Instead, Jim needed to build a structure and culture around Mark to ensure continued success and growth.

Jim knew the industry and saw the shifts in the market and the competition. He expressed concern that he missed an opportunity to shift the business a couple of years earlier. He felt the pressure from his Board to retire, delegate, and transition others to manage the company's clients. He had not built a sales team within the organization and the competition caught up while consumers began doing business differently in the 21st century. The company's numbers were slowly declining; actuals lagged behind quarterly projections and clients slowly departed for competitors. The end of Jim's career was not the script he had written—and he was anxious to rewrite a new chapter to the story.

His goal and focus now was on Mark and developing the necessary leadership skills and surrounding him with the right team to move the business forward, pivoting and transforming the way they do business. Jim and Mark had very different strengths and styles and it would be a fun, challenging journey to help Mark realize his superpowers and leverage those in this new role as the CEO.

The next 12 months became an amazing journey for Jim as he created a terrific legacy. He transitioned with grace as he empowered and supported Mark, surrounding him with a talented senior leadership team that complemented his strengths. Then, Mark and his team scaled the family-owned business beyond what anyone could have expected—a true Final Four moment for the father and son—and has seen its revenue grow to $700 million.

The 12-month road to transformation was not easy. However, not only did Jim learn to let go and to place trust in Mark, but he redefined his own purpose and meaning and chose the legacy he wanted to leave. Despite the expected challenges, we continued to collaborate and always circled back to the core purpose of sustaining and improving the business. Their impact extended beyond enhancing the business through a smooth transition; the way Jim and Mark enacted the transition made a positive difference for their employees' and clients' lives. They brought increased value to every stakeholder internally and externally, leveraging purpose-driven leadership and enabling fulfillment for every employee at the family-owned business.

* * *

To reach optimal personal and professional performance, we cannot just choose one or two competencies and expect to reach our peak. Developing the whole person—body, mind, emotional well-being, and purpose—puts all the puzzle pieces together. If we are missing any of these pieces, there will be a large and, at some point, the puzzle falls apart.

As corporate athletes, these gaps are magnified. Expectations are increasing and the stakes are high. *Which pieces of the puzzle do you excel in? What pieces of the puzzle represent major gaps for you?* Coaches develop and integrate these strategies and competencies into elite athletes' lives through daily routines and training. Today, these skills carry greater importance and weight for our overall success than our knowledge, technical skills, where we attended school and our résumé. No one is perfect and it is not easy. It takes a mindset, a plan, discipline, motivation, and daily practice. Eventually, these skills become natural habits and part of your routine as you start to experience more success and greater happiness.

Commit today to develop and strengthen these areas in your life. Are you ready to take action and move forward?

MASTER YOUR MINDSET: Your Inner Elite Athlete

+ In what areas—physical, mental, emotional and purpose—do you excel?

+ Which one(s) represent gaps and what is your game plan to improve them?

+ What lasting legacy would you like to leave personally and professionally?

10

Resilience Building Blocks

"Resilience is knowing that you are the only one who has the
power and responsibility to pick yourself up."
–Mary Holloway–

Can we claim to possess resilience? Is it a trait that we
have or do not have, like being short or tall? Fortunately,
resilience is not a born or static trait—it is dynamic and
can change. Top performers have a mindset that enables them to
overcome what seems impossible and to defeat the unthinkable.
When we are expected to perform every day in every role to the
best of our ability, our mindset is the key to success.

Walking the Talk

We often say that great minds think alike, but we need tools
and strategies in order to be successful, not just thinking. We are

all leaders from where we sit or stand; there is no waiting period for leadership. We lead from any chair, at every level in an organization, and in our own way. We are all leaders if we choose to "play" as leaders—leadership is a *contact* sport. Consider your work, home, and community life roles. *Where do you sit or stand as a leader, or choose not to lead?*

High-performing individuals share many common characteristics, but resilience rises to the top as the key element crucial to their success. Resilient people have the ability to sustain their energy level in a crisis, perform consistently under pressure, and manage stress to cope with and adapt to disruptive changes. They do not just perform when conditions are ideal, they thrive even when facing barriers and threats that off-track most of us. In order to survive and advance, we must have the ability to cultivate and strengthen resilience ourselves.

Personal resiliency represents a critical component as we interact in life and as we learn to lead effectively. True grit is not how we perform during the good times, but rather how we display emotional strength, courage, and professionalism during the most trying times. Leaders should study their teams, knowing and understanding their strengths and gaps, preparing them to succeed no matter the circumstance. Strengthening our personal resiliency clearly falls on each of us individually, but it is also our responsibility to build resilient teams and organizational resilience.

Resilience can be learned. While it will take significant effort and continual attention, the process will make us better than we were before. With resilience backing us up, we can live our lives with grit and determination . . . and find lives full of hope and happiness.

As emotional intelligence takes root in the minds of those who want to lead happier and healthier lives, they commit to live with resilience and determination. There are five key building blocks to develop and to strengthen personal resilience. Embracing the skills to place these building blocks for our foundation, we can generate a new limitless path forward and enjoy our journey with courage, confidence, and competence.

Building Block #1: Self-Confidence Is Contagious

Self-confidence leads off in the batting order for the resilient individual. Positive self-regard starts a rally of well-being that contributes to peak performance. Maintaining a mentality of ambition and possibility requires us to looking at ourselves in the mirror and express gratitude for the gifts and talents we possess. We cannot stand in self-reflection simply wishing for the best—performing at our best requires us to adopt a winning mindset about who we are and what we wish to accomplish. We must define our true north and crafting the personal values by which we live during our journey. The discipline to self-reflect and reinforce our self-regard also builds stamina and endurance, like the skillset of an elite competitive athlete.

Confidence is the difference between a winning streak and losing streak. The top coaches and leaders can help individuals become the best of the best and also get their teams into a winning rhythm—feeling empowered, unstoppable, and confident. Yet, if you have ever been in a slump or lost several games in a row, like a sales professional who receives multiple "no's" on the sales path and is unable to close deals, you may feel frustrated, lost, or insecure. My corporate clients and senior executives, as well as their teams, now have strategies and roadmaps to help them thrive. Many of them are expected to turn around programs and teams, recover from missed earnings, and turn around organizations quickly. For them, confidence is not an option, but a requirement.

We all need confidence to manage stress and to navigate turbulent times. Over the past three decades, my basketball coaching approach focused every day on instilling confidence in everyone. Successful athletes and coaches must be able to bounce back from losing streaks, defeat negative self-fulling prophesies, and overcome destructive thoughts and behaviors. As a coach, I expect to put individuals and teams on a winning trajectory and help them develop capabilities to do it on their own eventually. Striving to develop unflappable self-confidence and instilling it others is why many coaches do what we do. We know that resilience becomes limitless when confidence is on point.

Elite athletes experience degrees and cycles of confidence and understand that building and sustaining confidence requires a lot of work. We have all seen athletes who experience a little success, then a little more, and it continues as the game, season, and career progresses. Their eyes get bigger, their faces light up, they play more aggressively, take more risks, achieve more success, and move on quickly after making mistakes. In the simplest sense, these athletes just start believing in themselves. As a coach, seeing confidence that produces transcendent performance is inspiring and rewarding.

> *Successful athletes and coaches must be able to bounce back from losing streaks, defeat negative self-fulling prophesies, and overcome destructive thoughts and behaviors.*

I have worked with men and women—business leaders from the front line to the C-suite—who experience these same degrees and cycles of confidence and the roller-coaster that comes along with it. We all experience these variations in confidence. While there are many ways to develop it, we also must ensure it does not wane when we call on it. The ability to move on quickly to the next play or presentation, after making a mistake or failing, is the ultimate goal. It takes time and focus to build confidence.

Becky was one of the most confident players I had ever coached. Everyone wanted to be around her, on and off the court. Confidence is contagious, and her teammates figured that out. The more they were around her, the more mojo they accumulated and more confident they got. Becky had a vision for herself and for the team. She talked about it with passion; she inspired and excited others and she walked the talk. Becky was confident in herself as a person, student, and player because she believed in preparation. She was not the most talented player, but no one worked harder. She was in the gym before practice officially started, she stayed after for extra workouts, and she put in the time to watch countless hours of film of herself and our opponents. Her preparation gave her the confidence and an edge that readied her for the competition, mentally and physically.

Part of Becky's preparation for practice, games, and even a big exam, was establishing a routine and rituals. This strengthened her confidence and gave her great focus. For example, she always arrived at the gym an hour and a half before game time. She changed into her uniform, put on her basketball shoes, and tied her hair back in the same way every day, practice or game. She followed a shooting routine on the floor with one of our managers and she forced herself to make a specific number of shots from each spot. She sat in the same chair for introductions, high fived each person at the scorer's table, wiped her shoes on the sticky mat, gave all of her teammate's high fives in the same order, and then ran out to touch the 3-point line. After all of that, she walked towards center court and was ready to start the game.

Routines and rituals, like Becky's pre-game, instill the focus, discipline, and confidence that we need to perform at a high level consistently. Every elite athlete prepares and has their routines to get in their optimal zone. Do not get me wrong; Becky did not have a perfect game every night, but her routine gave her confidence, knowing that she did everything she could to prepare and to perform at her best. And when she made an error on the court, her confidence helped her move on quickly and get back into action.

Inside her locker, Becky posted her individual game and season goals. She displayed them so she could see them every day when she arrived at the gym. She set short-term goals that gave her the important opportunity to celebrate short term successes. During a long season, those short-term goals kept her on-track and she placed a gold star next to the ones she accomplished. It is important to reward yourself, and her gold stars served as a visual reminder to build confidence in tackling her long-term goals. Becky was not the most talented player on the team or in the conference, but she knew her strengths and values and became one of the toughest and best players on one of the best teams in one of the best conferences in the country.

We can learn from Becky's proactive and positive approach. Confidence builds and thrives when you have a vision for yourself, understand your strengths, recognize what you like about yourself, and celebrate your accomplishments. In preparing for your own success, setting short-term goals and celebrating small successes fosters and nurtures confidence. If you are leading teams, the leader as coach must accept responsibility to help their teammates develop and instill confidence. Confidence is how the best become the best—and continue getting better and better.

Building Block #2: This Little Light of Mine

As a child, whenever anyone asked me what I wanted to be when I grew up, I always replied, *The happiest person in the world!* My parents and siblings probably saw me as either someone starting too early on a path of purpose and meaning or as just a really strange kid. Most of us pursue happiness, yet most base their happiness on conditions. What makes each of us happy varies widely—from person to person and over time—like how we define success in our own lives.

Throughout my journey from child to collegiate athlete to coach, I wondered about my purpose and how I had gone so many years without hearing much about it. I define it simply as the light: the realization or fulfillment of one's talents and potential. Whether we know about it or make an intentional commitment to it, purpose resides within each of as an elemental drive or need. It is the highest of human needs to achieve one's full potential and to understand our why and meaning in life.

On the very top of Abraham Maslow's five-level Hierarchy of Needs rests Self-Actualization. We all can accomplish more than we think we can, mentally and physically. Unlike the other four Maslow needs that focus on securing something from our external environment—sustenance, safety, love and belonging, esteem—the self-actualization need emanates from within and drives us to see how much we can learn and grow from the inside-out. Learning and development positively impacts our resilience, strengthens confidence, and increases our overall outlook in our lives. When I reflect on my life, I realize that I have always had this trait. My drive and ambition for growth and development energizes me to strive to achieve at my highest level. My pursuit of purpose, meaning, and self-improvement is the light that brings me much joy.

> *Learning and development positively impacts our*
> *resilience, strengthens confidence, and increases*
> *our overall outlook in our lives.*

At one point during my collegiate coaching career, I decided to bring in an external expert who would work with my staff and team to identify our individual and team strengths. We used the *Gallup StrengthsFinder* and it was a great experience. I still leverage those results and self-awareness today in my coaching and my life. I learned that my number one strength was Belief, and that people strong in the Belief theme have certain unalterable core values. Out of these values emerges a defined purpose for our lives.

I have reflected on these lessons for years and I often return to this stage of my growth; it helps me understand my "why", how I am wired, and where my energy originates. Belief to me means that I have enduring core values, integrity, dependability, and consistency, and I deeply and fervently hold ideas about life, purpose, and how things should be. While I accept my number one strength of Belief, I am also aware how its practical manifestation may not serve me well in certain situations. For example, my belief is so strong about certain ideas and ways to approach life that when they are challenged, like in a debate with a friend or colleague, I know that I may need to walk into the other room to regroup. However, this knowledge also pushes me to learn to ask questions, to listen actively, and to affirm the righteousness of the other person's position.

When striving for self-actualization, happiness results from a willingness to learn and grow on a journey that aligns with your values. Let me be clear: sustainable satisfaction results from *learning* and *growth*, not from short-term achievement and accomplishment. My level of self-motivation and feelings about an enriched life ultimately drive life achievement and resilience. I can pinpoint the emotions I experience when I feel like I am optimally using my talents. *Can you?*

Not only do I draw happiness from personal growth, I am motivated intrinsically to reach my potential. In other words, my desire emanates from within, not from external validation. The people I hired, the players I recruited, and the clients I choose to work with today share similar goals and drive. Surrounding yourself with others who strive for life-long learning is motivating. We need these types of providers in our lives; it is fulfilling and energizing when such people challenge and push you to be your best in all aspects of your life.

So, if self-actualization means realizing our greatest talents and achieving our greatest potential, how do we do that? How do we achieve self-actualization? Those who are committed view growth as a tool to help others, not just oneself. Because resilience requires a spirit of continual improvement, this means we must foster a sense of learning, growing, and nurturing self-confidence. These truths are self-evident and connected in theory as well as practice. While they are independent aspects, they integrate to solidify limitless resilience.

Building Block #3: A Hopeful Future

Yogi Berra, the legendary, colorful, and former New York Yankee baseball player and manager is credited with saying, "When you come to a fork in the road, take it." For many of us, this type of faith can represent a defining moment in our lives. No one knows for sure what lies ahead, what lurks around the corner, or waits over the hill.

Sometimes, we must go on faith and belief in the possibility of a positive opportunity—which may reward us for our faith or become a learning event. In either case, know that with faith and a positive outlook and mindset, it will be ok. Optimistic people can look on the bright side and maintain a positive attitude in the face of setback and disappointment, and they have the ability to regroup, learn from the setback, and achieve happiness.

Early in my career, I became a young Division I head basketball coach at the age of 28. I learned so much during my first four years as head coach at the University of Vermont, a small Division I school where we enjoyed tremendous success. However, our Catamounts could only advance so far in the NCAA tournament at that level. I wanted more. I wanted to work at a school with the opportunity to win a national championship. After a final successful season in Burlington, I chose that fork in the road and took a career chance that I believed one day would propel me to reach my vision. It was a risky decision many of us face but often are afraid to take. However, to reach our dreams, we often must choose to take an unprecedented path.

Over the next five years I took what many considered a step back in my career to serve as an assistant coach at a prominent institution in a Division I power conference. I dedicated five years at Boston College competing in the Big East against some of the perennial powers every game and every year. It was very hard to take a step back from head coaching to an assistant's role and it affected more than just my title—it affected my prominence, ego, and role. As an assistant, I was not calling the timeouts or plays anymore; it was very difficult at first but I worked hard and stayed positive. I optimistically believed that working hard, learning, and performing my role to the best of my ability—if we were successful—would ensure interest in me as a next head coach at a school that could compete for a national championship and get to a Final Four. I chose to bloom where I was planted.

> *Optimistic people can look on the bright side and maintain a positive attitude in the face of setback and disappointment, and they have the ability to regroup, learn from the setback, and achieve happiness.*

Rather than feeling hopeless and losing faith, I stayed optimistic, believed in the process and my decision, and kept a realistic "can do" attitude. I stayed focused on my belief that things happen for a reason and good things happen to good people. After five years of working hard, developing my skills and knowledge, and preparing myself for my dream job, I got the call. It was the opportunity I wanted, and it met my vision. At the age of 36, I become head coach at a Big Ten institution, the University of Minnesota.

We can learn and strengthen our optimism with an intentional focus on looking at the brighter side of life, recognizing "what's right" instead of "what's wrong", and remaining positive in the face of adversity and life-changing events. The scientific research studies show that optimistic people live longer and have fewer illnesses and lower blood pressure. In a recent study published in the *Proceedings of the National Academy of Sciences* by Lewina O. Lee, Peter James, et al (September 10, 2019), optimism specifically related to 11% to 15% longer life span, on average, and to greater odds of achieving "exceptional longevity" (living to the age of 85 or beyond). In addition to the health benefits, optimistic people tend to achieve greater success in all their activities.

Typically, optimistic leaders lead resilient companies filled with optimistic people. Being able to communicate and inspire a sense of possibility when taking over a losing program or a depleted sales organization, optimism and a sense of possibility is a powerful message and tool. Be careful not to wear rose-colored glasses all the time; it's important to make sure we do not have a distorted sense of reality and we are tuned in and see things objectively in the moment.

Building Block #4: Life's Greatest Rewards

Building relationships is considered a key leadership capability. Many leaders fail because of their inability to develop interpersonal skills and meaningful relationships within their team and throughout the organization. When we have more mutually satisfying relationships in the workplace, we experience greater satisfaction with our jobs, higher levels of engagement, increased happiness, and fortified resilience. Most of our happiness develops in the context of our relationships with others. Mentors who support growth positively communicate with, connect with, and effectively coach others. Achieving our individual and organizational goals relies on nurturing employees to achieve their highest levels of performance.

Well-developed relationships help shield and buffer us from the negative effects of life's daily demands. Many of us feel fulfilled for the most part, but there are times when we all desire and need more encouragement and support. Most of us spend more time with our work families than with our families at home; we work a "normal" 40-hour week but often spend less than 40 hours with our kids and our spouse. Meaningful relationships in the workplace are critical for our happiness and engender greater resilience during tough times.

When we experience challenges at work, such as poor leadership or culture deficits, we feel unhappy and fed up with our workplace. But people who respect and appreciate their co-workers tend to get along and create a sense of belonging no matter what challenges they face, typically resulting in employee retention and longevity. We feel as though we can lean on our team and trust them, which is a crucial part of our overall workplace satisfaction, well-being, and culture. Organizations must continue to focus on creating this culture and environment with employees, particularly with so many working from home virtually.

> *Building trust, communicating effectively, demonstrating accountability, and staying connected take having a plan and strategy, made more difficult in a virtual world.*

Building trust, communicating effectively, demonstrating accountability, and staying connected take having a plan and strategy, made more difficult in a virtual world. Because the expectations of business growth and performance remain unchanged, this must continue as a critical focus for leaders. As leaders, we must bring positive energy to our teams to offset the fatigue and stress of trying to stay engaged, whether under typical conditions or during unusual circumstances.

Clearly, coaches and players benefit from developing good relationships, particularly trusting relationships. On and off the court, we set goals and accepted the responsibility to create a great experience for our players. We nurtured their growth through their experiences, successes, and failures while teaching them life lessons during their formative years. As coaches, we recognized relationships contributed significantly to players' mental and emotional wellness. Building trust with parents, high school coaches, and others who were integral in players' lives also was important for the coach-player relationship. In the business world, Gallup employee engagement studies reaffirm annually that the relationship we have with our supervisor is the reason people stay with or leave a company—not compensation or other tangible benefits. Taking ownership for healthy relationships is everyone's responsibility.

As the operational expression of emotional intelligence, relationship building relates strongly with the desire to cultivate social skills and meaningful relationships, as well as the ability to feel comfortable and authentic. Take some time and write down any particular relationships at work you can improve to increase harmony. Ask yourself these two questions:

Do I feel as connected as I need to be with my team?

If not, what steps can I take to improve the relationships?

This is a start and is usually part of my coaching sessions with my clients. Relationships and the trust we develop are a key to resilience.

Building Block #5: Doing the Right Thing

I have the heart of a philanthropist with a drive to give back and to pay it forward. We all express philanthropic desires and we each give differently; I founded two nonprofits but you might serve on a board, take an active role in church, volunteer your time, or donate money or goods. Take a look at what is inside your heart. Giving of ourselves to others is one of the five building blocks to strengthen our resilience.

A desire for social responsibility originates from generosity, empathy, and compassion for others. When you have this kind of heart, the extent of what you give matters less than your attitude, motive, and behavior. When you give of your own personal resources, you choose to commit your time, accept others, and leverage your talents and theirs for the good of the collective community, not just yourself. This creates a strong sense of fulfillment and becomes who you are.

Most of us have the desire to influence and to make a difference in others' lives, either within your organization and/or in the community. You become an influencer and promoter of others, create an awareness that shapes the organization, adds value to society, and also changes the perspective of others. In addition, when we give back, we set an example of concern for the welfare of others, sending a positive message to those around us. Integrating yourself into the community and expressing a desire to make things better is a refreshing demonstration of emotional intelligence.

> *Purpose-driven companies—such as those that emphasize the "triple-bottom line" of profit, people, and the planet—often are more successful. They attract the best minds, they have passionate stakeholders, they bring value, and they strive to change the world.*

Mother Theresa gave more of herself to her chosen causes than any other public figure of our time, devoting her entire life to the world's most oppressed people. High-profile coaches and professional athletes make a substantial amount of money each season. Besides creating foundations or donating a percentage of their salaries to charities, making personal appearances, and adopting families over the holidays, they serve as roles models and set an example in which their communities take pride. In most organizations of the past, there was no designated opportunity for social responsibility. In the 21st century, a big part of a company's culture involves giving back, encouraging community service hours, and even providing paid time off for volunteering. Purpose-driven companies—such as those that emphasize the "triple-bottom line" of profit, people, and the planet—often are more successful. They attract the best minds, they have passionate stakeholders, they bring value, and they strive to change the world. The company's impact is powerful, not only for individuals, but also on the public as they advance the entire ecosystem.

Increasing our commitment to social responsibility is the easiest of the five building blocks to strengthen resilience. It is also the easiest component of emotional intelligence we can change. Being socially responsible can happen even on the smallest scale, helping one person at a time. A high level of this competency means a better and more fulfilling life. *What have you done recently to help those in need? How does this make you feel?* Find ways to give back and to help others and enjoy the satisfaction you receive in return.

The Ideal Coach and Teammate

Many leaders make the mistake of not coaching and developing their people and teams. If you have facilitated your team members to a point of independence you have met a goal most leaders do not achieve. All leaders should strive to be coaches; for the leader-as-coach, mentoring, motivating, and developing others is an evergreen task. Continue to work with new team members to increase their level of responsibility and they will grow, improve, and gain confidence steadily. Your goal is to "work yourself out of a job" so when it comes time for you to move up to greater responsibility or move on to a new challenge, you have people who can step in, take your place, and lead your team without skipping a beat.

We all have an obligation and responsibility to be an ideal teammate in our organizations. Ask yourself these questions:

How do you define "being a team player"?
Can your team depend on you?
How do you know this is the case?

What are some examples of where your success can be attributed to your team and not you alone?

Resilience will continue as a hot topic in our lives, in leadership, and in business, and companies will seek resilient individuals when hiring top talent. Many individuals do not know themselves well enough to determine if they have a high level of resilience or not until after the fact. You can and should test for it—it matters in business and in our lives. A person's level of resilience determines their success and how they handle the pitfalls and detours along the way. Resilience differentiates successful people in life, in sports, and in the boardroom.

The five building blocks for resilience, fully teachable and learnable, represent actions to commit to now. An increased level of resilience correlates to mental and physical health. Resilient people are realistic optimists; they possess a strong belief in their purpose and meaning and they have the ability to quickly adapt. To truly maximize resilience, focus on these five critical building blocks and stick to it.

* * *

Adversity, setbacks, and disappointments in our lives test and impact our resilience. During the pandemic, social unrest, the divisive election, and the financial crisis many of us face, our resilience tank may sit on empty or it may run on fumes. We can fill up our tank by practicing and integrating these actions into our lives daily.

MASTER YOUR MINDSET: Your Building Blocks

✦ Which of the building blocks represent strength(s) for you? How will you leverage those strengths?

✦ Which of the building blocks represent gap(s) for you? What will you do to fill them?

✦ What (a) personal and (b) professional experience(s) have you had that tested your resilience? How did you hold up? What did you learn about yourself?

11

Resilient Teams

"People want to be on a team. They want to be part of something bigger than themselves and feel they are doing something for the greater good."
–MIKE KRZYZEWSKI –

My teams would out-work, out-hustle, and out-last our opponents. Laser focus and purpose in all aspects of preparation underpin a strong work ethic. I learned this on the farm, refined in The Barn on campus, and applied it in the boardroom. Many times, the difference between success and failure came down to grit and grinding to get through tough times. While I had certain a way I wanted things done, I learned through a talented coaching staff to lean on others for their expertise. Our team's Final Four experience never would have happened without the contributions of a great staff—and the tight teamwork of our players. We came together like a chain, with each link integral to the other and producing an unbreakable bond.

Playing the Way You Practice

I wanted everyone associated with the Minnesota Golden Gopher program to learn, to grow, to develop, and to improve constantly. We practiced with the intent to improve and to get better, individually, and together. Our coaches designed drills and practices in response to watching game film, using scouting reports, and finding the little things that paid big dividends. I often told players that doing the right thing when nobody is watching ensures your legacy of honor and respect. Our approach fostered a common purpose and shared leadership; I could not know or do everything. And, while my coaching staff demonstrated tremendous competency in this regard, we welcomed and needed informal team leaders to step up—and they did.

It all came together through our relationships, fueled by straight and direct two-way feedback. You know the kind: honest, timely, and constructive so you can improve in real time. When each player, coach, and support staff member deeply commit to have each other's back, the result is the real power of a high-performance team. The commitment extended to every day and every moment on and off the court, and every practice and game situation, through a heart-felt commitment—not just when it is easy, convenient, or selective on a given day. This mutual win-win covenant and team agreement rested on a foundation to communicate authentically and with care and to support each other in every situation.

Additionally, we practiced and coached to have a focused mindset of resilience. Learning to manage failure and have a short memory about losing with a long memory about winning inspires a willingness to do what is required to compete. This empowered us to show up strong for practice and games and to overcome adversity. My personal motto for living these beliefs was asking myself each day, *What am I doing today as the head coach to master my mindset?* It all came together with a can-do attitude that fortified our resilience and mental toughness.

We all must take personal responsibility to manage our own personal resilience at home and at work. It is impossible to achieve positive mental health or to realize our dreams without taking personal responsibility seriously. Accept it or not, we all are responsible for the quality of and course of our lives, without blaming others or allowing external barriers to off-track our efforts. We have the power to choose. Taking personal responsibility for our lives can be tough; it requires the willingness to take risks and action, while acknowledging and learning from our mistakes.

Most of us work on one or more teams. For many leaders, building high-performing teams means turning team development on its head. While accountability for personal resilience rests with us, behaviors with and between our peers add to or detract from our efforts. Unwritten rules and unspoken perceptions may shape the outcomes for team development; we may be clear about our purpose, but others around us may have a different version or understanding. We must overcome these barriers and shift team development to perform optimally and to sustain success over the longer term.

While team goals and expectations must remain solid, frequent change demands team agility. Purpose generally remains fixed, yet the goals and the means of achieving them may need flexibility. Bureaucracy, complex processes, and fixed mindsets may block team success. In addition, inauthentic team behaviors can undercut a successful team's trajectory. For example, you may appear to have agreement around the table, yet team members may walk away and undermine what was decided or refuse to change.

Teams and leaders must commit to evaluation and improvement. After losing a game, failing with a project, or erring in execution, leaders must use these events as teachable moments and pursue opportunities for growth. The analysis and learning of an "After Action Review", popularized by military branches in the U.S. Department of Defense, serves as a great opportunity for a team to take the time together, to reflect carefully, and to debrief about what went well and what they can do differently next time. These meetings must feature a healthy balance of team successes with missed opportunities, celebrating the positives and specifying what can be done better next time. Leaders should encourage their team members to speak up and to raise any relevant concerns they have about the event. And they should recognize and show appreciation for those who lend their voices to the learning.

Teams must do more with less. Regardless of the industry, efforts to meet this suffer when expectations of deliverables often do not balance with resources. To combat this situation, teams must use their team members' strengths and skillsets to build a culture of continual improvement. It also requires regular communication to prioritize and to decide where to direct collective energy. And sometimes, a collection of resilient individuals does not guarantee a resilient team. Teams must adapt and work together in productive ways, learn from success and failure, and support each other under all circumstances.

Team Dynamics

According to research from RallyBright, just two percent of teams rise into the category of "resilient". Only two percent! Resilient teams regroup and generate strategic solutions when setbacks occur, which seem to appear more frequently in the workplace these days. Common setbacks include changes in leadership, mergers and acquisitions, furloughs and layoffs, departing and new team members, under-performers, poor leadership, and global threats such as health or economic crises.

> *Resilient teams seek feedback on how they are performing and build on what is working well. Then they work together to address opportunities for improvement.*

In your team, what happens when a problem arises? How do you respond? Is there collective effort and ownership or are people left to solve their own problems? Resilient teams leverage appreciative inquiry and past peak performances emphasize possibilities optimistically and focus on solutions collaboratively. In a landscape of frequent change and chaos, teams need to ensure they can continue to deliver consistently through strategy, competitive, and industry shifts. Resilient teams seek feedback on how they are performing and build on what works well. They establish a culture that emphasizes coaching, mentoring, providing peer support, and understanding different learning and communication styles.

Stress and change often lead to teams breaking down into cliques or independent individuals, and some may pull back from the team concept in attempt to cope personally. While an understandable human behavior, this limits individuals from performing at their best and prevents the team from achieving high performance. A defensive response from a team member often slows down learning and makes the entire team less resilient, negatively affecting team performance. Support, belief, and positivity characterize resilient teams and team members during times of change and stress.

I have seen many leadership teams hit by several crisis the last few years, for many reasons. In one example, several team members responded to the stress and uncertainty by taking individual positions—blocking others, competing for credit, and blaming others—in an attempt to survive personally. The team under this stress broke down, rather than pooling their ideas and working together for a positive outcome. Overall team performance devolved into a disaster and, only after the adversity of failed team performance, the team attempted to re-build. At this late stage unfortunately, bridges were burned and several individuals left the company.

In sports, I consider these types of teams as "frontrunners", performing only under good conditions without adversity or strain. Studying film allowed us to quickly identify our frontrunner opponents; we knew these teams, when everything was going well, they were very hard to beat. But we knew, if we put pressure on them and built an early lead, or kept stress on them throughout the game, they would become frustrated on the court and collapse. They could not bounce back from adversity or move on to the next play quickly after a mistake. This happens for many business teams and organizations. Multiple stressful circumstances have hit us all and, for many, a dramatic and highly stressful response only delayed the inevitable collapse.

Leaders must build their teams and develop mindsets with a strong internal identity and a clear purpose. Leaders at all levels must demonstrate and value resilience. They set an example for their teams because all eyes are on them for direction and as a role model. Each team member looks to the leader to determine the behavioral norms to which they should aspire. When team members ask themselves questions—*What makes me feel safe?; Am*

I utilizing my strengths?; What makes me feel valued?—leaders who demonstrate personal resilience set an example of how their team members should behave and respond under stress.

Successful teams have a culture, ego, and brand of resilience. *Within your team, how are people who demonstrate resilience described? Do highlights and shared stories affect your team's resilience? Is there a common language for crisis, stress, and coping mechanisms and are these discussed within your team?*

Team Resilience

Resilient teams believe in each other, commit that teamwork comes first, adapt to adversity, and take risks. Legendary dynasties like the Montreal Canadiens, New York Yankees, Connecticut Huskies women's basketball, U.S. Women's National Soccer, and New England Patriots model these traits and leverage them, whether walking over a weaker opponent or edging a fired-up competitor. They perform with elite teamwork no matter the circumstances.

Resilient teams believe they can effectively work together and achieve success together. Beyond each individual's confidence in their own abilities, the team believes they can win at a high level together. The New England Patriots trailed by 18 points at half-time of Super Bowl LI but they dug deep and fought back to win their fifth title. They were a resilient team with the confidence and belief they could make enough plays to come back and win.

Teams with resilience have the mindset that teamwork comes first. All team members must get on the same page about their roles and responsibilities and manage their own and others' behaviors during good and bad times. This helps them coordinate, predict one another's behavior, and make decisions together on the fly. This mindset must be consistent to be effective—one without the other will not work. When inconsistent, some team members may not understand the plan or the play which may cause a delay in or mis-direction of their response. This scenario off-tracks teams during good times; during times of adversity, it crushes performance.

When team members share an understanding of execution tactics and how each other's roles fit, they can confidently carry out their roles to the best of their ability, without hesitation. It was critical that my players understood their strengths and their roles on the team. With 10 seconds to go in a game, when we draw up the winning play during a timeout, everyone must understand their own role quickly, within a 30-second timeout. Then, they all walk out of the timeout with confidence and a shared mindset to win. When the game is on the line, execution needs to be perfect in order to win.

Teams must adapt and develop new ways to handle adversity—their crooked rims—to build resiliency. To pivot quickly and effectively, teams need to access existing knowledge from past experiences and creatively develop new ideas when facing setbacks. Resilient teams become intimately familiar with one another's past experience, skills, and abilities so they can leverage each other's expertise at the right time.

Members who share a belief that it is safe to take risks enhance team resiliency. Such teams have members unafraid to speak up and to share creative ideas without fear of criticism or singling out by the leader or team members. Team members can share constructive criticism and feedback with each other and, instead of becoming defensive, they integrate it to get better. On resilient teams, the feeling of psychological safety enables members to voice their ideas and opinions openly and honestly. The safety of team expression leverages and engages the diverse perspectives that we all need to gain benefit.

Internal networks

Strategic, diverse internal networks help teams deliver on outcomes. When team members network widely within and outside of the organization, the access to knowledge, relationships, skillsets, and perspectives extends our teams' capabilities and ultimate success. Networking broadens a team's reach and resources without adding new team members. As expectations change, teams who network proactively stay relevant and competitive.

Besides my coaches and players, there was no group of people more critical to the success of my program than the athletics and academics support staff. Because these team members were not direct reports, I focused on building trust and relationships. The relationships and expertise of our academic advisor, strength and conditioning coach, trainer, sports medicine specialist, marketing director, and strategic communications, were dealmakers or dealbreakers. If one relationship went bad, our entire program suffered; managing these relationships was as important as winning games. These cross-functional relationships and resources were critical to our overall success, helped us win games, and strengthened resilience throughout the entire program.

How well is your team connected with others inside and outside the organization who can support your goals and success? Where are your resource gaps and how strong are your existing relationships?

Connectedness

Connectedness in a team operates as emotional glue. Team members care about each other, advancing a feeling of family and a sense of belonging. Connectedness fortifies a foundation that establishes trust and enables you to attract the best of the best. Talented people want to join teams and cultures that make them feel welcomed, important, valued, and safe. When this happens, confidence and comfort give individuals freedom to take risks without fear of mistakes.

A 2017 Accenture study of more than 1,100 American workers—yes, before the global pandemic relocated nearly everyone's workplace to kitchen tables and living room couches—noted that remote employees are more likely to feel left out and ganged up on than their onsite colleagues (*Harvard Business Review*, November 2, 2017). Specifically, they worry about bad-mouthing by workers behind their backs, project changes without their input, and lack of support for their priorities.

In addition, the study identified, through feedback from more than 800 of the respondents, seven skills for managers to make their remote employee feel included and cared for:

1. Check in with distant colleagues regularly and frequently
2. Insist on some face time (even via phone or video conference)
3. Practice exemplary communication skills such as active listening
4. Make expectations explicit
5. Be available to remote colleagues through a variety of channels
6. Demonstrate familiarity and comfort with technology
7. Prioritize relationships and emphasize team building and camaraderie

A culture and environment of connectedness is essential to grow any team. *What does connectedness look like (or not) on your team? What happens in the team to show empathy and value for people?*

Team Optimism

Besides needing energy and perseverance to reach our goals, optimism has become more important as our environment has become more difficult. Positivity brings power and it promotes overall well-being and resilience for the team. Leaders must notice and acknowledge work ethic, attitude, and progress in celebrating individual and team success together, while constructively and openly acknowledging reality and opportunities to improve.

Work by researcher and high-performance team consultant Marcial Losada demonstrates the power of team positivity. In one study, he identified the effects of negative emotions in the work setting, observing behavior in company meetings behind a two-way mirror. He measured the proportion of positive to negative statements, self-focused versus other-focused, and inquiry (appreciative) versus advocacy (position-taking).

From further work studying teams of eight while they developed strategic plans, he developed the Losada Ratio—a positivity ratio represented by the sum of the positivity in a system divided by the sum of its negativity. He found that a ratio of 3.0 to 6.0 correlated highly with high performance, through quantitative (tangible) outcomes like profitability and qualitative (soft) measures like evaluations by colleagues and superiors. Losada measured and found that high-performance teams have a 6 to 1 ratio of positive to negative statements, while low-performing teams were under 1 to 1.

While negativity can tank a team quickly, blind optimism also can erode team performance over time. *How is negativity addressed within your team? How are successes acknowledged as the outcome of a team effort? How do you manage individual egos and agendas that can negatively impact a sense of collective effort?*

Building Team Resilience

Resilience represents a latent capability that strengthens future performance, called upon when conditions require the toughness to overcome difficulties. Because leadership drives culture within the team, leadership effectiveness will increase or decrease your team's resilience. If your idea of resilience training and development focuses primarily on individual employee well-being, you run the risk of relying on a valuable workshop or presentation with a short-term, unsustainable impact for team performance.

Developing resilient teams takes time, focus, and discipline. Maximizing impact requires aligning a long-term commitment and approach, leadership development, and business strategy. Success derives from a combination of solid leadership throughout the team, effective communication and continual collaboration, and team members who understand one another and work well together. We do not need every team member to be a superstar to excel.

Today's constantly changing environment creates a greater demand than ever before for resilient teams. Leaders and managers fulfill the key role to foster resilience within their teams. *Within your team, who is on point watching your resilience antennae? What are they doing to facilitate greater resilience?*

Leading With Coaching

Leaders are integral to employee growth, development, and satisfaction on a continual basis. They must find ways to connect in powerful ways that truly matter. When team members feel valued and supported by their managers, stress and anxiety levels decrease and performance and results increase. Managers must develop into leaders and leaders must become coaches.

Dr. W. Edwards Deming, a renowned organizational quality and performance guru in the 1950s until his death in 1993, wrote in *The New Economics* (2ⁿᵈ Edition, 1994) about the "role of a manager of people". A few of his 14 points about the role include that managers are unceasing learners, act as coach and counsel not as judge, use knowledge and tact as sources of power, create an environment that encourages freedom and innovation, and listen and learn without passing judgment. Deming also is reported to have responded to a CEO who asked for a meeting with him with a letter simply stating, "Come yourself [the CEO] or send no one." Leaders must step up and lead the transformation. There is no proxy or delegation for leadership.

Resilient teams are more important to businesses than resilient individuals; while individuals build resilience independently, leaders must carefully cultivate team resiliency through collaboration with team members. Resilience separates successful individuals from the rest, from an entrepreneur who finally succeeds in the marketplace after numerous failed attempts, the scientist who produces a life-saving vaccine after years of failed trials, to the basketball player who overcomes a severe injury or a shooting slump to advance to the NCAA tournament. However, none of these individuals would succeed without other members of their teams.

Very few of us work entirely alone, and how our team perseveres really is what matters. *What role do leaders play to help resilient individuals come together in your organization to become a resilient team?*

Winners Make Pit Stops

Teams have their foot on the accelerator constantly, as our environment rewards and demands forward progress. Yet, despite the need for speed, no one decision is any bigger than taking the time to make a pit stop to assess, to regroup, and to recharge. When a NASCAR vehicle pulls into the pit stop, the pit crew works in harmony. They remove five lug nuts from each tire, all of which go flying. A single mistake by the pit crew can put a team as much as a lap or two behind, if not more. Their driver and the team sponsor rely on them to perform flawlessly in front of crowds and to deliver results in seconds.

We can learn a lot from a pit crew on how to develop and perform as a resilient team. Everyone must know their role and do it better than anyone else. The entire team depends on everyone and the team must prepare for anything to happen and to adjust. They operate in sync, in a rhythm, and they focus with laser sharpness at exactly the right time. The pit crew practices and prepares for the worst-case scenario. They understand that they stand in the gap between winning and losing. While the driver gets the victory lap, they are the unsung heroes.

These necessary timeouts also provide real-time feedback among the entire team about overall performance. This precious time allows for race-time adjustments that may be required to keep competing and to win the race. During the brief pit stop, the pit crew engages together with shared purpose, vison, and values. This requires a resilient coach who understands and role models being a resilient individual first, before expecting others to form a resilient team.

The NASCAR driver who achieves the winner's circle recognizes the collective efforts of all stakeholders for his success. *How does your team take purposeful pit stops to learn, to regroup, and to recharge?*

* * *

During my time as Minnesota's head coach, it was critical for us to build resilient teams every year and we worked hard doing it. Now I enjoy the rewards of helping and supporting leaders in developing resilient teams and strong cultures in business. Our basketball team changed every year; for many in business your team changes even more frequently. Each team member must collectively buy into the purpose, team values, and their role. Our team culture, mantra, belief, mojo, and mindset were that no one would ever out-work, out-hustle, or out-physical our team. We would prepare better and achieve greater fitness than any other team. No matter who we played, where we played, or the time of year, our competition knew they had to bring their A+ game and be ready to battle. We carried this brand and ego like a badge of honor.

My work with many teams and team members demonstrates the benefit of a strategy and road map to help build and to support a culture of team resilience. It must become a team strength, rather than a roadblock. The hard work takes a strong commitment, but the payoff accrues to your team and you will build a lasting legacy and set yourself up for long-term success.

MASTER YOUR MINDSET: Your Resilient Team

+ On your team, what happens when a problem arises, from initial reactions to problem-solving?

+ What are the characteristics of the best team you have ever been on?

+ How does your team build resiliency and how is that demonstrated?

12

Mental Toughness

"Watch your thoughts; they become words.
Watch your words; they become actions. Watch your actions;
they become habit. Watch your habits; they become character.
Watch your character; it becomes your destiny."

−LAO TZU−

Mentally tough athletes can step up in the most competitive situations, pulling through when pressure mounts to perform consistently at their optimum level. Trust me, mental toughness does not always look perfect or excellent. Sometimes, even the most mentally tough take a step back before moving forward. Mental toughness exemplifies a mental ability to manage stress and to replicate consistently what is required under difficult circumstances. It takes resilience to the next level.

The Toughness Differentiator

Stakeholders, boards, and leaders expect mental toughness from the corporate athlete: demonstrate exceptional performance, climb the ladder, stay relevant, and innovate in your industry. The corporate athlete's role requires mental toughness like the elite athlete, if not more. Whether an individual contributor, team member, manager, senior level leader, or executive, we all want to be surrounded by fierce competitors whose mental toughness lifts performance to the next level.

As a head coach for many years, I learned a lot about hiring and recruiting fierce competitors for my staff and team. We had extremely high expectations and expected a lot from the program every day, week, month, and year. You need these same qualities when you build high-performing teams. I have worked with many leaders who want to transform their teams into driven, high-performing, fierce competitors. As a coach, there were years that I took passive, fragile, and entitled athletes and turned them into focused, disciplined, and mentally tough team players and successful teams.

Mentally tough coaches and players who can transition from the sports world can have an unmatched impact and success in another career. Many former athletes and coaches join, build and manage enterprises as "retired" coaches or athletes. The lessons we learn from becoming the best at our sport carry incredible value into other aspects of life and business. The relatively short span of an elite athlete's career—roughly 10 to 15 years—generates a lifetime of experiences, learning, and growth. Stepping off the court into the business world takes mental toughness to transfer winning skills and to produce as much if not more success for others.

Mental toughness drives success in multiple ways. An elite athlete—in sports or business—must handle pressure, have unwavering self-belief, and avoid outside distractions. They must know they have all the capabilities to achieve anything they desire and possess an indefatigable desire to win, no matter the circumstances. These traits separate good athletes from the elite at the collegiate and professional levels and differentiate between a good and elite corporate athlete.

The Toughness Challenge

Coaches learn quickly that players need mental toughness to get through the daily grind of college athletics. And coaches understand that they must intercede when necessary; I discovered that ignoring drama, problems, and challenges would not make them go away. I had to learn to work through the many different challenges until I found solutions that I could help my players implement.

Yet, after I retired from coaching college sports, I still found myself surrounded with general life challenges—ones I could not ignore just because they were hard, uncomfortable, and inconvenient. In addressing these challenges, I found that I needed to draw on the same mental toughness I had developed as a college coach to break through the new and varied obstacles and unknowns in my new path.

People misunderstand mental toughness. Too often, it is associated with a tough or fixed mindset that refuses to bend or to break. This simplistic view is not true. Mental toughness is the ability to manage our emotions and to control our thoughts and behavior in ways that set us up for success. We are not born with mental toughness—it is a trait we can learn and cultivate, and not only during tough times.

The hardwired brains of human beings typically react first with emotion. No matter how tough and in control we think we are, we tend to express emotion particularly in difficult situations. Following the emotional surge, we have an opportunity to take total control of our mindsets. If we achieve control, we have the power to manage our emotional reaction and address the situation optimally.

I have developed relentless competitors for almost 30 years at the NCAA Division I level and prepared many of my players to continue in the pros. It is an art coaches must develop daily no matter what is going on in our lives. There were days that we did not play the way we needed to compete. Given the conference and the schedule we played, we had to show up and compete every single night over the grind of a long season. Besides mastering my own mental toughness, I expected the entire coaching staff to have each individual and the entire team ready to compete relentlessly every day.

> *Our hardwired brains typically react first with emotion. No matter how tough we think we are, we tend to express emotion—particularly when facing difficult situations.*

Business leaders are becoming increasingly frustrated by the lack of drive, competitiveness, and toughness in the workplace today. Rather than working hard, going above and beyond expectations, and focusing on the job right in front of them, many team members are looking for what's next. This leaves senior-level leaders trying to figure out how to lead in a culture of entitlement and looking for the next promotion.

Many professionals come into the workplace today thinking they deserve rewards regardless of producing, working hard, or competing for them. We have all seen such individuals enter the competitive arena, and when things do not go their way, they blame someone else for their shortcomings. These individuals give teams no chance to reach their potential and to get to the next level. Resilience and next-level toughness take a back seat.

Clarity of Vision

I will share a few techniques that helped me become a fierce competitor and a mentally tough coach. First, I learned the importance of solidifying my own vision and articulating it to others. While most people must discover their life purpose, a few others come out of the chute with clarity of purpose and vision for their life. I was one of those lucky few. It was clear to me when I turned 21 years old and I kept my eye on the ball from that point forward. Most others are not as fortunate, and I now realize most people struggle to figure out what they want to do and what vision they have for their lives.

Before we identify our vision, we must answer a bigger question: *How do I discover what is important to me?* Mental toughness requires clarity of vision about yourself and where you are headed in life. Identifying it ignites a fire in our bellies and gets us excited. To determine what is most important, we start by taking inventory of the activities that we love, digging into our passions, and acknowledging the impact we want to make on the world and people around us. We search ourselves, our experiences, and our hopes and dreams to discover the "essence" of what drives our deepest satisfaction and gives us energy. Then we can formulate a clear vision for the life we want to live and take action to accomplish it.

It takes discipline and perseverance to not settle for complacency and mediocrity. Instead, we pursue significance and meaning in our work. Importance differs for each person and it is easy to settle for the status quo of a steady job or stable career that may not create passion. Mentally tough people discover what they want from life and take the actions they must to make it happen. If you desire more from life, take time to get clarity.

Out-working Everyone

Like any important intangible in the sports world (leadership, commitment, confidence, character, unselfishness), it is much easier to enhance and refine an existing trait than to develop it from scratch. The best way to cultivate mental toughness and build fierce competitors is to use it as a key characteristic in recruiting and hiring. Of course, we all need talent, but I searched for players from winning programs because I knew they came from competitive cultures and knew how to win. You can ask candidates to describe situations that placed them under stress and to explain how they reacted initially, how they adjusted, and how they succeeded. Then ask them to relate a situation they could not overcome, and how they felt, coped, and moved forward.

It is important to create a healthy competitive culture to challenge and to drive your team. To improve and to foster competitive drive, you must consistently push yourself and others outside the comfort zone. Experiencing and managing discomfort teaches us how to toughen up and eventually to "break" our opponent or the situation. Playing it safe or avoiding discomfort serves only to hamper us when the going gets tough. We must commit to out-work anyone, anytime, no matter what.

Leaders as coaches help instill a competitive attitude in their teams. They set the expectation that pressure is a privilege every day and that team members must give their best. The most successful leaders are caring yet driven and have high expectations in a healthy way. You must find that fine line between pushing team members to achieve their potential without pushing them over the edge. When they learn to compete and to surpass their own expectations and barriers, they will have the confidence to soar and to thrive at the next level.

Tracking results really brings out the competitiveness in people. One of the pivotal moments in my life came in the fifth grade when my teacher wrote the names of the eight students with the highest grades on the blackboard. I looked up at the list and my name did not appear on it. That list remained on the board for six weeks and the next time the teacher updated it, I made sure my name was there. As coaches, we meticulously tracked the results of practices and games and posted them to motivate the team. In business, my most successful clients use dashboards, key performance indicators, and quarterly targets they need to hit. They work with team members to establish targets and stretch goals.

No matter the talent level or industry, these strategies worked for me in the sports arena and they work in business. At General Electric, famed CEO Jack Welch required his business units to rise to the top in each market they served—and when they reached number one or two, he made them redefine the market so they would not drop but redouble their efforts to climb back up on the leader board. If you find yourself or team at the bottom, do something about it. Encourage team members to make a decision to fully commit to work harder and smarter and create healthy competition to get the best out of your team. When you do, you will develop a mental toughness mindset in everything your team sets out to do.

Research and case studies show that mental toughness increases performance up to 25 percent in your goals and production. Mentally tough performers show greater commitment to purpose and they are more competitive. They grow and develop more, meet deadlines more consistently, manage stress better, achieve greater satisfaction in life, and are less likely to develop mental health issues. They demonstrate optimism and a "can do" attitude and are more ambitious.

Mental toughness for individuals, teams, and organizations is immensely important, especially in times of chaos and when the pace of change is rapid. Leaders, high potentials, and those working in stressful, unforgiving industries or in situations of uncertainty, must develop and cultivate a mentally tough mindset.

Goals and Values Alignment

Once we identify the important work, the next step involves setting goals to help move you in the direction of your vision. If you need resources for setting goals, there is no shortage of coaches, self-help books, and gurus willing to offer their expertise.

When our goals and dreams are big, it is often hard to know where to begin. Do not feel bad or guilty if you miss a goal; I miss my stretch goals at times (but still make great progress). Chasing goals to satisfy your deepest passions will motivate you to persevere and not to give up. Our passion and values represent the best of yourself.

Values differ for everyone, but it is critical to dig deep and to uncover those that will lead you to personal growth and close relationships. If your goals do not align with what is most meaningful to you in life (your purpose and vision), make changes to align your values into your daily life. Then set your goals and get to work.

Mental Toughness Mindset

The non-stop chatterbox of our minds may sound like a cheerleader, encouraging us to move forward, or a bully, becoming our own worst enemy. While we prefer the positive messages, sometimes our minds react with fear when the unknown confronts us because its job is alert us to danger ahead.

Science demonstrates the power of positive thinking, which goes hand in hand with mental toughness. Learned optimism is a mindset that must be developed and cultivated. The next time an obstacle or roadblock confronts you, remember to flip the script and to change the message in your mind. Do not look at a roadblock as permanent; it is only a temporary impediment. Rather than an unavoidable obstacle, think about it as a unique situation that you cannot wait to attack. Instead of taking things personal and making it all about you, develop an "it's-not-all-my-fault" attitude. Accept responsibility for part in the situation, but do not beat yourself up about the elements outside your control. In the game of life, mastering our mindset matters.

The grit of a mentally tough mindset separates the best of the best and average performers in their respective fields. Many people who end up at the pinnacle of their careers are not the most talented or gifted. They are the ones who put in the blood, sweat, and tears. Do you know underachievers and overachievers? The world is full of them. Choose to overachieve and start by strengthening your mental toughness. Here are a few techniques we instilled in our elite athletes to develop their mental toughness:

- Learn to take responsibility for your actions and hold yourself accountable, do not blame others or make excuses
- Consistently challenge yourself to be the best and to get better
- Learn not to take failure personally and to use it as fuel and motivation
- Develop confidence in your own strengths and abilities
- Set short-term and long-term performance goals and then go after them
- Strengthen their confidence to manage self-talk during the most difficult times

- Leverage visualization and mindfulness for emotional and mental strength

We can all develop and maintain this level of mental toughness required for success. It is crucial to keep our thoughts positive and to avoid habits and patterns that lead to negative and unhealthy behaviors. The strongest people are not those who outwardly display strength and toughness in front of us, but those who win the internal battle and private fight when no one is watching.

* * *

Do not wait for a tough situation to test your mental strength; put these strategies into play now so you are ready at any moment. Choose to lift your resilience to the next level by mastering a mental toughness mindset. Over time, you will have mastered limitless skills to apply in your life and leadership as a mentally tough, positive thinker.

MASTER YOUR MINDSET: Your Mental Toughness

+ How will you leverage the traits that enable, or improve those that undermine, your mental toughness?
+ What is the vision or purpose for your life? How are you sharing it with others, making it a reality, and holding yourself accountable?
+ What techniques will you embrace to lift your resilience to the next level and develop a greater level of mental toughness?

CONCLUSION:

Your Final Four

*"If you learn to use it right—the adversity—it will buy you a
ticket to a place you couldn't have gone any other way."*
–TONY BENNETT, UNIVERSITY OF VIRGINIA
MEN'S BASKETBALL COACH–

When you step into the arena of your life and the
lights go on, your Final Four opportunity awaits.
Will you be ready? Will you handle the pressure
and remain focused? Will you marshal your mental resilience and
physical strength and perform at your peak?

As I wrapped up writing this book, mixed emotions wash
over me: joy and excitement, anxiety and nervousness, and many
others. I experienced a similarly thrilling and nerve-racking emotional roller coaster during our team's journey to the Final Four.
I approached every March Madness tournament with gratitude

because I knew deep down that getting there involved a process and a journey filled with humor, frustration, victories, defeats, and feelings of tremendous accomplishment. Despite the emotional whirlwind, I learned to enjoy the most exciting tournament of the year, March Madness, just as I appreciate the exhilaration of finishing my second book. When we value the hard work it takes to achieve these milestones, it produces amazing gratitude.

College basketball players or coaches who reach the Final Four experience a dream come true. Whether dribbling on a shiny gymnasium floor or hoisting shots at a crooked rim tacked to an old barn, every player and coach grows up and hones their skills with thoughts of the Final Four in mind. It is euphoric and the greatest sporting event of the year, bar none. March Madness transforms even non-sports fans into diehard fanatics. For whatever reason, we love our March Madness brackets. ESPN estimates that Americans fill out 70 million March Madness brackets each year, enjoying the competition with their friends, families, and co-workers and tracking their bracket game by game for three weeks.

One amazing realization is that very few head basketball coaches ever get to experience guiding a team to a Final Four. Most coaches will never experience this amazing leadership and coaching achievement, and I never took reaching the Final Four— the pinnacle of my career—for granted. It was never an easy road. To achieve this level of success in any sport, a team must have an exceptional leader and each member must demonstrate personal resiliency. The leadership skills and relentless resilience coaches need to develop resilient teams, also are required in the workplace to lead five generations of workers. With a high level of resilience, adaptability, and inspirational leadership, you will have the same euphoric experience of reaching your own Final Four.

How do we get tougher than our competitors? As a coach, I sometimes forgot to define toughness. Now, I am focusing on mental toughness, framing it by understanding what it takes to "break" a person. Coaches often talk about what it takes to break a player and sometimes design training and practice to break down individual players and the team. It is like deciding if you will board up a beach house's windows or put hurricane windows on them. *Can the house and windows withstand a serious storm? What type of windows are strong enough to stand up to the storm? What does it take to break them?*

What does it take to break you in your life? Legendary University of Connecticut Women's Basketball Coach Geno Auriemma said, "With the absence of pressure, it is hard to do great things." It doesn't matter what circumstances you are faced with, when you face pressure, you should ask yourself, *What does it take to break my focus?* When you get frustrated, anxious, or stressed out—when the last play did not go your way or someone gave you feedback you did not want to hear—*will you give in or break?* When conditions have made you tired and overwhelmed, and you do not feel good, you may not be able to give your best effort. *What does it take to break you?* Especially now as we face adversity in our personal and professional lives, we need to know what it takes to break us . . . so we can work hard to build the resilience it takes to thrive.

As you commit to training, developing, and learning new skills, prepare yourself to perform at the next level. Corporate athletes must ready themselves to endure whatever life and work throws at them. You will face personal and professional crises, uncertainty, and chaos while constantly adapting to evolving norms and navigating uncharted waters. You will be asked to develop new skills and level up in order to have capabilities that are lacking today and are necessary for success tomorrow.

Everyone needs to develop and strengthen mental toughness to achieve and to sustain next level performance. If you fail or make mistakes, fail with grace; do not let it affect the "next play" or your ability to move forward. Developing a short memory and letting mistakes go will help you maintain your confidence at peak levels and build mental toughness. If you let mistakes affect you, you allow frustration to break you. When my players missed a shot, forgot to box out for rebounds, turned the ball over, or messed up their timing on a play, or I subbed them out of the game without an explanation, *Did it break their resilience? What does it take to break yours?*

No easy path forward will present itself; you must put in the work to develop the toughness you need to face each crooked rim and excel. I have always emphasized the importance of discipline; what I have learned over time is that mental toughness is a key ingredient for discipline to do what is expected. Mastering your mindset, strengthening your resilience, and developing mental toughness will minimize the circumstances that can affect your ability to accomplish what is needed at any given moment.

We have all experienced peak performances in our lives—times when we were totally "in the zone" and firing on all cylinders. Think about a time when you were operating in a peak performance state, a time when your expectations, skills, and goals all lined up and you experienced your own Final Four. We all can experience our own Final Four personally and professionally, so think about how that looks and feels for you. Leaders are expected to inspire their teams to reach their Final Four by defining it and having a game plan. Work the plan, enjoy the process, celebrate the successes along the way and execute the strategy to get there. When you do, make sure to enjoy the journey and . . . then set your sights on your next Final Four!

Resilience is a capability learned through experience and earned through effort. We all can develop courage and strengthen the toughness required to achieve anything we can imagine. To be the hero in our own lives—and to lead others to success—we must discover who we are and what we are made of on the journey to master our mindset to strengthen resilience. Then, no matter what crooked rims we face, we will overcome them and will experience our own Final Four. And our lives will feel and be limitless.

MASTER YOUR MINDSET: Your Final Four

✦ What does it take to "break" you and your spirit? How can you demonstrate mental toughness when facing adversity?

✦ What Final Four(s) do you want to reach personally and professionally? By when?

✦ What actions will you take to achieve your Final Four(s)?

ACKNOWLEDGMENTS

In some books, acknowledgements can feel a bit rote. For me, sincere acknowledgements are extremely important as an expression of my deep gratitude.

Our lives are a journey and I have been blessed my entire life with the people I surround myself with and also others who are gone. None of us arrive at our destinations without those around us who have impacted us in so many ways. There are so many people to thank because I surely did not get here myself.

I offer my deepest gratitude to:

- My wife, Lynn, who has influenced my work more than ever, and your support and love are gifts beyond measure.
- My clients, who have become my second family, providing me with real-life lessons, challenges that keep me on my toes, real-time learning, and feedback. They also have been some of my biggest cheerleaders with encouragement, ideas, and accountability, without which I could have never written this book. My clients are now my players in my life today. They are my fuel and the reason I do what I do. I have learned as much from you as you have learned from me.
- Adam Cohen, my book editor and much more, for your amazing insightful ideas and edits throughout the process, on matters large and small. Adam thoughtfully applied his writing and creative talents, business strategy experience, and love for sports to shape this book.

- James Doyle, who deserves a heartfelt thank you for helping me write this book. He believed in me from the first time we met at a coffee shop, two strangers brought together for a reason. We met weekly for months, enjoyed walks around Lake Harriet, explored my personal and intimate stories, and discussed his views as a father and professional. Jim is a man of undeniable hope who gave me a whole new perspective on life.
- Mom, Dad, and my family. Your love lights my life and put me on the path to my life's passion to help others succeed.
- All of those who supported me during the writing of this book with words of encouragement I needed many times throughout this journey.

I will continue to use my gifts to make a difference and create impact in the lives of others for as long as I live.

ARE YOU ON POINT?

Pam Borton is the Chief Executive Officer and Founder of On Point Next Level Leadership, a firm dedicated to changing lives and helping individuals, teams, and organizations experience their own Final Four. On Point Next Level Leadership provides executives, executive teams, team leaders, managers, and employees with everything they need to enable high performance for their teams and organizations, perform as one team, and elevate people to the next level.

Visit www.onpointnextlevel.com.

Resilience and Well-Being Coaching and Training
Executive Coaching
Speaking
Team Coaching
Leadership Academies
Books

ABOUT THE AUTHOR

As a leading International Coach Federation (ICF) Master Executive Coach, professional speaker, and author, Pam Borton is committed to taking C-suite executives, teams, and organizations to the next level. She partners with organizations across the country including financial services, retail, manufacturing, hospitality, technology, law enforcement, healthcare, media services, military, insurance, physicians, and more.

In today's culture and environment of constant change and disruption, building successful leaders and high-performing teams is an expectation. Pam provides her clients with real business experience navigating high-level challenges and complexity in the workplace. Her background stands apart with 27 years of Division I women's basketball coaching, including 12 years as head coach at the University of Minnesota in the Big Ten. There, she led her teams to a Final Four, Elite Eight, three straight Sweet Sixteens, and numerous NCAA Tournament appearances.

As the CEO and Founder at On Point Next Level Leadership, a boutique leadership consulting firm, Pam uses her unique skills to help organizations tackle issues such as improving organizational health, building high-performing teams, leading with grace under fire, executive and leadership presence, leveraging emotional intelligence, strengthening resilience, and managing change.

Pam is a philanthropist at heart and has founded two nonprofit organizations in Minneapolis, Minnesota. She launched TeamWomen in 2011, a nonprofit organization dedicated to empowering women through mentoring and professional development. In 2015, Pam founded a second nonprofit—Empower Leadership Academy—providing youth in grades 5-12 the tools and support they need to become the next generation of leaders.

Pam's work and life have been recognized with several awards including the 2016 *Twin Cities Business* Magazine Marvelous Mentor Award, Top 10 Global Women of Leadership Pillar Award, (Real) Power 50 Award, and New England National Coach of the Year. She was also a two-time nominee for the Naismith National Coach of the Year Award. Additionally, Pam was honored with the creation of the Pam Borton Endowment at the University of Minnesota in the College of Education and Human Development, the only endowment of its kind in the world. In 2019, Pam was inducted into the National Association of Women Business Owners (NAWBO) Hall of Fame in Minnesota.

Pam has achieved multiple certifications and degrees:

- National Board-Certified Health & Wellness Coach (NBC-HWC) where she implements executive wellness, psychological wellness, and mental health strategies in the corporate world, law enforcement, professional and college athletics, and future leadership of our youth today
- ICF MCC (International Coach Federation) Master Coach Certification
- Advanced Certified Personal and Executive Coach from the College of Executive Coaching, Santa Barbara, California
- Certified Global Team Coach (ITCA)

- National Board-Certified Health & Wellness Coach (NBC-HWC), by Physicians
- EVERYTHING DiSC Trainer Certification, Wiley
- EQ-i 2.0 and EQ 360 Certification Training, College of Executive Coaching, Santa Barbara, California
- The Five Behaviors of a Cohesive Team, Wiley
- Certified in Positive Psychology and Well-being
- Certified in Hardiness Resilience Gauge (HRG)
- B.E. Organizational Change Leadership Certification
- National Women's Business Enterprise Certification
- M.Ed., Sport Management, Bowling Green State University, Ohio
- B.A., Physical Education & Science, Defiance College, Ohio

A free ebook edition is available with the purchase of this book.

To claim your free ebook edition:

1. Visit MorganJamesBOGO.com
2. Sign your name CLEARLY in the space
3. Complete the form and submit a photo of the entire copyright page
4. You or your friend can download the ebook to your preferred device

Morgan James BOGO™

A **FREE** ebook edition is available for you or a friend with the purchase of this print book.

CLEARLY SIGN YOUR NAME ABOVE

Instructions to claim your free ebook edition:
1. Visit MorganJamesBOGO.com
2. Sign your name CLEARLY in the space above
3. Complete the form and submit a photo of this entire page
4. You or your friend can download the ebook to your preferred device

Print & Digital Together Forever.

Snap a photo

Free ebook

Read anywhere

CPSIA information can be obtained
at www.ICGtesting.com
Printed in the USA
JSHW020146041221
20976JS00001B/11